Sea Charts of the
BRITISH ISLES

Haven

pendenis

Trefuses poynt

Sea Charts of the
BRITISH ISLES

A Voyage of Discovery Around Britain & Ireland's Coastline

JOHN BLAKE

Foreword by Admiral of the Fleet, the Lord Boyce KG GCB OBE DL

ADLARD COLES NAUTICAL

BLOOMSBURY

LONDON · OXFORD · NEW YORK · NEW DELHI · SYDNEY

Author's Acknowledgements

I want to thank my editor, Alison Moss, for the second time, for guiding and steering me clear of difficulties, and to my Publisher, John Lee, for suggesting the book and trusting me to write it. This book is intended to appeal to the interested public at large, rather than the academic, and I have therefore left out specific references, but these can be supplied by me through the Publishers.

A number of maritime archives supplied the images and gave me much help: Matthew Sheldon, Head of Research Collections, at the Royal Naval Museum in Portsmouth, along with Allison Wareham, Librarian and Head of Information Services; Guy Hannaford, Archive Research Manager, Ann Browne, Archive Research Officer, and Helen Breeze, Archive Marketing Manager for Commercial Development, and The Admiralty Collection® at the United Kingdom Hydrographic Office (all UKHO images are reproduced by permission of the Controller of Her Majesty's Stationery Office and the United Kingdom Hydrographic Office, www.ukho.gov.uk); Geoff Armitage and many of the staff at the British Library Map Room and Sandra Powlette in the Permissions Department; Paul Johnson, The National Archives Image Library Manager; Brian Thynne, Curator of Hydrography at the National Maritime Museum, London; Dr Tony Trowles, Librarian at the Library of Westminster Abbey, London; Dr John O'Neill, Curator of the Hispanic Society of America, New York; Mark Myers at the Hartland Quay Museum; and Ian Rippington and William Wilson at Imray, Laurie, Norie & Wilson Ltd.

My thanks go also to many who have helped me on the wider aspects, including Captain Rodney Browne CBE RN (former Captain of the RN Hydrographic Survey Squadron), Robin Harcourt-Williams, Curator to the Marquess of Salisbury at Hatfield House, Dr Andrew Cook, Map Archivist, India Office Records, and Stephen Swann, Editor of *Traditional Boats and Tall Ships* magazine.

I am grateful, too, to my wife, Francine, for her patience and support.

This book is dedicated to my 5-year-old grand-daughter, Gabriella. May she and all young children be able to enjoy our coastal heritage in its natural and unspoilt state.

Adlard Coles Nautical
An imprint of Bloomsbury Publishing Plc

50 Bedford Square   1385 Broadway
London   New York
WC1B 3DP   NY 10018
UK   USA

www.bloomsbury.com
www.adlardcoles.com

ADLARD COLES, ADLARD COLES NAUTICAL and the Buoy logo are trademarks of Bloomsbury Publishing Plc

First published 2005
This edition 2016

© John Blake, 2016

John Blake has asserted his right under the Copyright, Designs and Patents Act, 1988, to be identified as Author of this work.

British Library Cataloguing-in-Publication Data
A catalogue record for this book is available from the British Library.

Library of Congress Cataloguing-in-Publication data has been applied for.

ISBN: PB: 978-1-4729-4490-0

2 4 6 8 10 9 7 5 3 1

Design Anna Pow, Margaret Brain
Printed in China by RR Donnelly Asia Printing Solutions Limited

Bloomsbury Publishing Plc makes every effort to ensure that the papers used in the manufacture of our books are natural, recyclable products made from wood grown in well-managed forests. Our manufacturing processes conform to the environmental regulations of the country of origin.

To find out more about our authors and books visit www.bloomsbury.com. Here you will find extracts, author interviews, details of forthcoming events and the option to sign up for our newsletters.

Contents

Foreword by Admiral the Lord Boyce GCB OBE DL, Lord Warden of the Cinque Ports and Constable of Dover Castle 7

Introduction 9

| HALF TITLE PAGE | ISLE OF EDAY BY HORATIO NELSON HESS, 1821 | Eday is one of the smaller Orkney Islands in the middle of Sanday Sound with Sanday Island a mile to the north and Stronsay Island a mile to the south. (UKHO © British Crown Copyright)

| FRONTISPIECE & TITLE PAGE | FALMOUTH HAVEN IN THE LATE SIXTEENTH CENTURY | Lord Burghley, as Elizabeth I's Lord Treasurer, and concerned to advise her best as to the defence of the Realm, needed a visual idea of how the vulnerable southern coast looked, and this manuscript plan of Falmouth Harbour gave him a good idea. For good measure the fleet is shown sailing south and already a galleon is engaging a Spanish ship in Falmouth Bay, while the standards are raised in the two fortresses, Pendennis and St Mawes Castle, built by Henry VIII at the entrance to Falmouth Haven. (By permission of the British Library: Royal 18D.III)

| RIGHT | THE NEEDLES BY STAFF CAPTAIN J PARSONS, C. 1830 | The infamous chalk rocks at the westernmost point of the Isle of Wight known as the Needles have become the graveyard of many ships all but home after a long voyage.

The present lighthouse, 109 feet high, built on the base of the most westerly rock of the Needles group, started working on 1 January 1859, taking over from the original lighthouse on the cliff top. The light, 80 feet above high water mark, can be seen 14 miles away at sea level. (UKHO © British Crown Copyright)

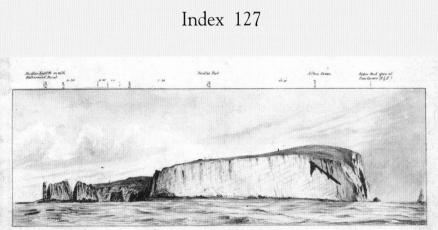

| DOVER HARBOUR, C. 1531–2 | As one of the original Cinque Ports, Dover is the traditional base of the Lord Warden and Admiral of the Cinque Ports at Dover Castle. The other four are Hastings, Sandwich, New Romney and Hythe. As they began to silt up, they had to enlist adjacent ports to fulfil their obligations to the Crown, which declined after the Tudor navy was established, of providing 57 ships with 21 crew for 15 days a year. Other ports brought in as 'Corporate Members' were Deal, Ramsgate, Faversham, Folkestone, Margate, Lydd and Tenterden.

The Italian engineers Vincent Woulfe and Vincenzo Volpe were asked to look at improving Dover in 1543, with the building of their proposed moles (breakwaters).

In fact, the great mole that we can see today with an eastern and western entrance was built at the instigation of the Admiralty at the end of the nineteenth century when, under the pressure of German re-armament that culminated in the First World War, they selected Dover as a minor naval base. Before the moles were built, Dover, although dominated by the Norman castle, was a beach port. Today it is one of Britain's chief ports handling ferries to France and a large amount of commercial cargo. Dover has prominence, too, as one of the selected 'standard ports' for high and low water time and height predictions in the Admiralty Tide Tables. (By permission of the British Library: Cotton Augustus I.i.19)

The Constable's Tower
Dover Castle
Dover
Kent
CT16 1HU

In medieval times, one of the duties falling to the Office of Lord Warden of the Cinque Ports was the supervision of the coastal defences of the 'Invasion Shore' of England, and my predecessors ordered surveys and charts of the ports and coasts from which they could plan and direct England's defence from sea-borne attack. And during my career in the Royal Navy, I relied absolutely on the accuracy and reliability of charts both in command of HM ships and submarines, and subsequently in Flag appointments when directing naval operations.

During the eighteenth century, however, the Royal Navy was in an anomalous situation. It was generally winning naval encounters with the French - but often with French charts to guide them! France had the cartographic lead and was the first to set up a National Hydrographic Office, long before the British, in 1720. Its appearance, and the loss of a number of ships through shipwreck rather than enemy action, finally persuaded the Admiralty, and an Order in Council was signed by King George III to set up a British Hydrographical Office in 1795. This was not before time, particularly as Britain's doctrine of freedom of the seas under *Pax Britannica* after the Napoleonic War in 1815 needed a British Naval presence in all corners of the globe and, with that, the requisite charts. Admiral Sir Francis Beaufort, the longest serving British Hydrographer from 1829 to 1855, oversaw an extraordinary and ambitious endeavour to chart the coastlines of the world, and this was especially directed at our shores as a 'Grand Survey of the British Isles'. And whereas chart information had hitherto been kept a national secret by all maritime powers, to its credit Britain then made this information commercially available world-wide.

Charts today, of course, have mercantile and leisure usage, as well as defence, that is commendably fulfilled for the shipping and fishing industries, and the power and sailing boat enthusiast, by the Admiralty chart and other commercial chart publishers such as Reeds and Imray, Laurie, Norie and Wilson.

Sea Charts of the British Isles presents the story of surveys around our coasts and ports and how they were made, giving a rich illustrated insight from a panoply of charts going back to the sixteenth century from the archives of national institutions such as the British Library, the National Archive, the UK Hydrographic Office, the National Maritime Museum and the Admiralty Library in Portsmouth. It brings to the general reader an unusual angle to the history of what a previous Lord Warden, Sir Winston Churchill, called 'Our Island Nation'.

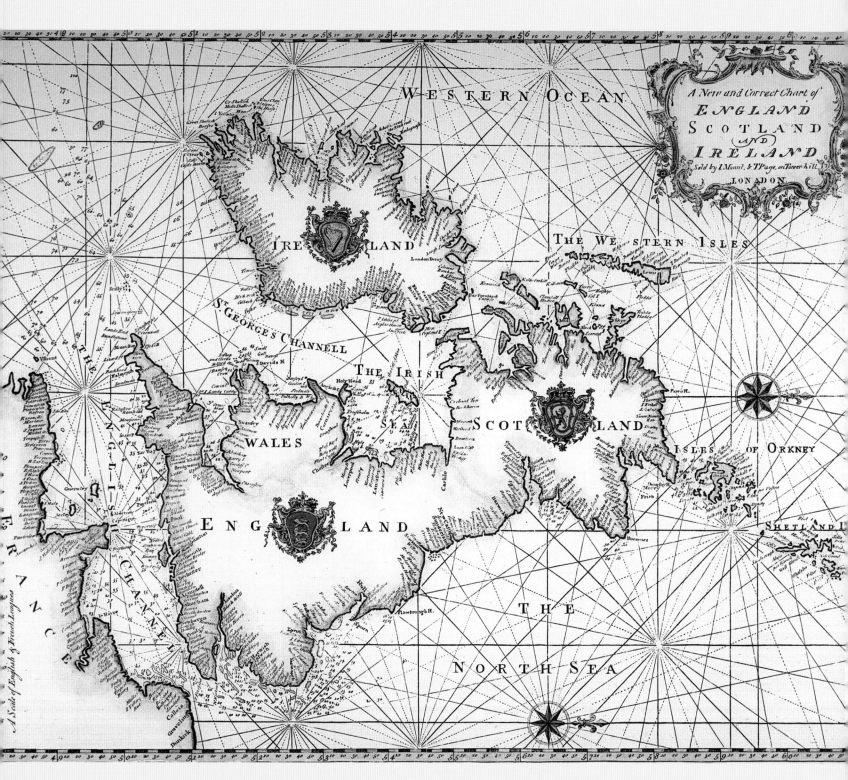

| CHART OF ENGLAND, SCOTLAND AND IRELAND, C. 1746, PUBLISHED BY MOUNT AND PAGE | Described as (they always were) 'A New and Correct Chart of England, Scotland and Ireland', this chart is constructed along the lines of the older portolans. It has a circle of 16 compass roses, each with 32 rhumb lines (lines with a constant compass bearing enabling a navigator to steer a course), and a square grid made up of parallel lines that join opposite centres of the compass roses. Each compass rose is placed exactly 2° of latitude (120 nautical miles) apart. This created a grid that brought a constant size of latitude but no longitude.

Richard Mount published the first edition of Greenvile Collins' *Great Britain's Coasting Pilot* (1693), and as Mount and Page, published John Seller's *The English Pilot* from 1698. (UKHO © British Crown Copyright)

Introduction

THE British Isles depend on the sea, but we who live here can suffer from sea-blindness, little realising how much our way of life is made possible through the ships that bring goods and food, export our manufactured products, and provide the naval defence of our island. We are shaped by our maritime past and Britain can celebrate centuries of maritime achievements. A vessel is vulnerable when navigating close to shore and a key instrument of its safe arrival in port has always been the chart, which has evolved over centuries with contributions known and unknown from numberless seamen, who learned their trade the hard way, through the unforgiving experience of the sea.

For landsmen, the coastlines of the British Isles have always held a fascination. Witness the growth of tourism over the last couple of centuries as families migrate for a summer holiday to seaside towns and fishing ports that, made increasingly accessible in Victorian times by the spread of the railways, have adapted to cater for them.

What is the attraction? I have been fortunate to be born and spend my formative years in seaside towns, in Brighton at school and Tenby in Pembrokeshire for holidays, in one of the richest counties for geological diversity in these isles, and I still love to go back. There is always a sort of primeval delight when the sea comes into view. The skeleton of the land is exposed and wild nature is on view.

This book offers the chance to view the coasts of the British Isles through the surveying pen of our maritime ancestors. I have taken a chronological and geographical slice from the enormous amount of charting material that exists in our maritime archives and museums to give an overall taste to the reader. Some may feel I have left out stretches of the coast or harbours important to them; forgive me, there isn't room to include them all. I hope the reader will be content, too, that when I refer to the British Isles and include the island that is Eire and Northern Ireland, I do so in the geographical sense, not the political.

My selection takes some of the earliest views and plans available from the sixteenth century through to the time when the coasts were first accurately charted during the mid-nineteenth century. Generally speaking, the maritime nation that held the ascendancy of power on the seas produced the charts that were used by the rest. Sea power opened the door to newly discovered land and resources overseas, and the chart was the key. Spanish and Portuguese portolan charts of the fifteenth and sixteenth centuries were more instruments of prestige and power, and were ordered and used by the monarch and aristocracy: they were never used in the way a chart is today, to plot and check the course of a voyage (although they would be used as a visual aid). These were superseded in accuracy and knowledge by the Dutch as they developed their Far East trade in the seventeenth century, and by France and Britain during their relentless maritime competition over the eighteenth century, culminating in the Battle of Trafalgar and a century of *Pax Britannica*.

Captain Thomas Hurd, who relieved Alexander Dalrymple as Hydrographer in 1808, wrote the first report on the State of Hydrography in 1815. He began:

The return of Peace to this country makes me consider it as an official duty to represent to the Lords Commissioners of the Admiralty the great deficiency of our Nautical knowledge in almost every part of the World...but the most remarkable of our deficiencies for our great Maritime Nation is our want of a competent knowledge of the contour and real geographic situation of many parts of our own shores...

This set in motion an ambitious strategy, welcomed by a navy that, due to the 'peace dividend' at the end of the Napoleonic War, had diminished from 125,000 to 23,000 men and was looking for employment, to survey the seas and coasts of the world, and particularly what a later Hydrographer, Admiral Sir Francis Beaufort, oversaw as the 'Grand Survey of the British Isles'.

Charts of the ports and harbours, and stretches of the British coastline, were drawn out of necessity – to guide trade, to review defence, even to define ownership. Although born of functionality, they are fascinating to our eyes in their naivety, or their artistic beauty, or the sheer amount of detail they contain, and all have interesting stories to tell. I hope the reader will enjoy this eclectic circumnavigation of these obstinately independent islands, perched in the Atlantic on the edge of Europe, geographically apart, yet joined by historic migration and cultural curiosity.

CHAPTER I

CHARTING THE
BRITISH ISLES

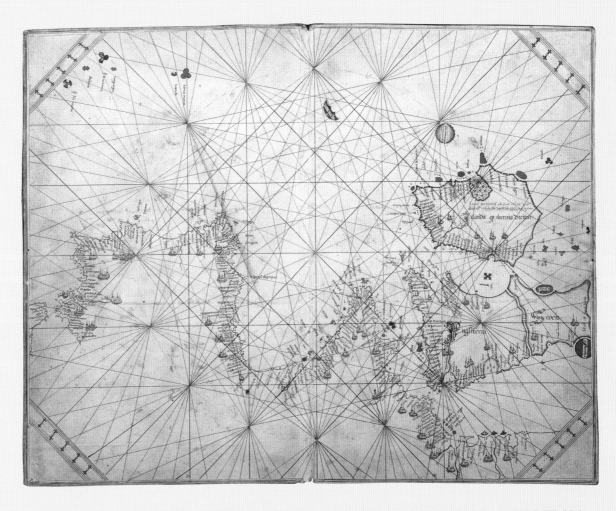

| LEFT DETAIL & ABOVE | PORTOLAN CHART OF THE NORTHERN ATLANTIC FROM SCOTLAND TO GIBRALTAR BY CONTE HOCTOMANNO FREDUCCI, 1537 | On this chart the British Isles and Ireland have still to mature to the real coastline, especially as Scotland is shown (as some may wish it now) as a separate island. It has been drawn on parchment in the typical portolan style, with 16 points equi-spaced around a circle, each with 22 rhumb lines (10 left out) and parallel equidistant lines drawn through opposing points, giving a grid on which to draw and measure the land's outline. (Courtesy of The Hispanic Society of America, New York)

WHAT did maritime surveyors of the British coastlines find when they surveyed her shores?

The British Isles reached their current position perched on the North Atlantic shelf some 20 million years ago. Between 300 and 180 million years ago, the super-continent known as Gondwanaland that straddled the equator began to separate in a north–south movement. By 100 million years ago the drift had changed to an east–west movement, so that by 40 million years ago the Atlantic Ocean was formed. By 20 million years ago the five continents were roughly in the positions we find them today.

The geology of the coastline of this island group is incredibly varied, reflecting the dramatic and often violent way the land was formed through volcanic activity, changing sea levels, and the impact of the ice ages, the last of which ended only about 10,000 years ago. Up to the end of this Ice Age, the nomadic tribes who wandered the European continent were able to walk across the dry bed of the North Sea until the melting ice filled the now sunken plain.

The cliffs around the islands change from grey and white limestone, red sandstone, white chalk, hard granite, soft clay, sand and towering columns of basalt. The limestone cliffs found around Tenby in South Wales, Llandudno's Great Orme in North Wales, Humphrey Head and Arnside Knott along the Lancashire-Cumbria border, Durness in Scotland and along the coast around Durham were formed as a sedimentary rock in the Cretaceous period some 100 million years ago from the shells of molluscs that were so abundant in the warm, shallow seas.
The chalk cliffs so reminiscent of southern England from Dover, past the famous Beachy Head to the Isle of Wight are
a soft form of limestone composed of the shells of tiny marine protozoan animals. The rock of Portland Bill, well known for the quarried stone that built St Paul's Cathedral, consists of Jurassic white limestone formed by the deposits from millions of seashells. Red sandstone cliffs, found in Pembrokeshire, Caithness and the Orkneys, are tougher but will eventually succumb to the relentless rolling of the waves.

The toughest cliffs are granite, an igneous rock that has formed as quartz, feldspar, hornblende and mica, which vary in colour from shades of pink, red, grey and blue to be seen in the Scilly Isles, and parts of the Cornish coast.

Another type of volcanic rock is found in the impressive basalt cliffs so characteristic of Staffa (Fingal's Cave) off north Scotland, the Giant's Causeway in Northern Ireland and many of the Hebridean islands, such as Skye, Mull, Muck, Eigg and Canna. Isolated stand-alone plugs of basalt where sea birds, such

| ABOVE | BEACHY HEAD, VIEWED FROM THE ENGLISH CHANNEL SOUTH OF DEAL BY C F OLDHAM, 1867 | This is a fine watercolour of a coastal view sent to the UK Hydrographic Office as the basis for engraving a chart navigational elevation of this part of the English Channel. (UKHO © British Crown Copyright)

as kittiwakes, fulmars and herring gulls, safely nest in profusion, were left behind from a complex of softer rocks, such as Bass Rock, that prominent fixing landmark for vessels going into and out of the Firth of Forth, and the Farne Islands, where puffins and guillemots nest, some 5 miles south of Lindisfarne or Holy Island, off the Northumberland coast.

The soft cliffs in Suffolk and Norfolk are of sand and clay, mixed with gravel, which are unstable and prone to landslips and erosion with the sea encroaching a few feet into the land each year. The people who live there have tried to prevent or reduce the extent to which the land is slipping away by building sea-walls, groynes and breakwaters, and embankments of sand to stop the sea's incursion, for example at the edge of The Fens.

To summarise in very general terms, mainland Britain consists of two basic kinds of rock: very old pre-Cambrian metamorphic rock to the north and younger igneous rock such as granite found in Cornwall, and basalt, to the south, delineated by a line from roughly Cumbria to Kent.

THE BRITISH ISLES

The British Isles is a polyglot of, unexpectedly, some 5000 islands. The largest of these is known as Great Britain not, as some die-hards might like to think, because of her Empire, but to distinguish her from Brittany or 'Little Britain'. Most of her inhabitants will know that this island is made up of the earlier realms of England and Wales, united politically, legally and administratively under Henry VIII in 1543, and Scotland, united by the Crown under James I (James VI of Scotland) in 1603, but only united politically after innumerable wars and unrest, by the Act of Union of 1707.

The other large island, now divided as the autonomous country of Eire, and Northern Ireland, a part of the United

| RIGHT | THE FIRST GEOLOGICAL MAP OF ENGLAND AND WALES WITH PART OF IRELAND AND SCOTLAND BY WILLIAM SMITH, 1815 | William Smith was the first to really understand the implications of the rock strata that make up the British Isles in terms of geological development. Born into a family of small farmers, as a boy he became fascinated by fossils. He learned geometry, surveying and mapping and was appointed to a master surveyor, Edward Webb, travelling the length of Britain in his work. Supervising the construction of the Somerset Canal for six years gave him the opportunity to study in great detail the rocks, and fossils, through which he had to dig. He noticed the order in which fossils always appeared enabling him to deduce a logic as to the rock strata, age and evolution. Eventually, with 400 subscribers, he financed publication of his map in 1815. It was to become one of Darwin's supporting props for his later theory of the evolution of the species. The map is dedicated to Sir Joseph Banks, the President of the Royal Society who had sailed with Captain Cook on his first Pacific Voyage. (By permission of the British Library: MAPS.K.Top.5.76. 6.TAB)

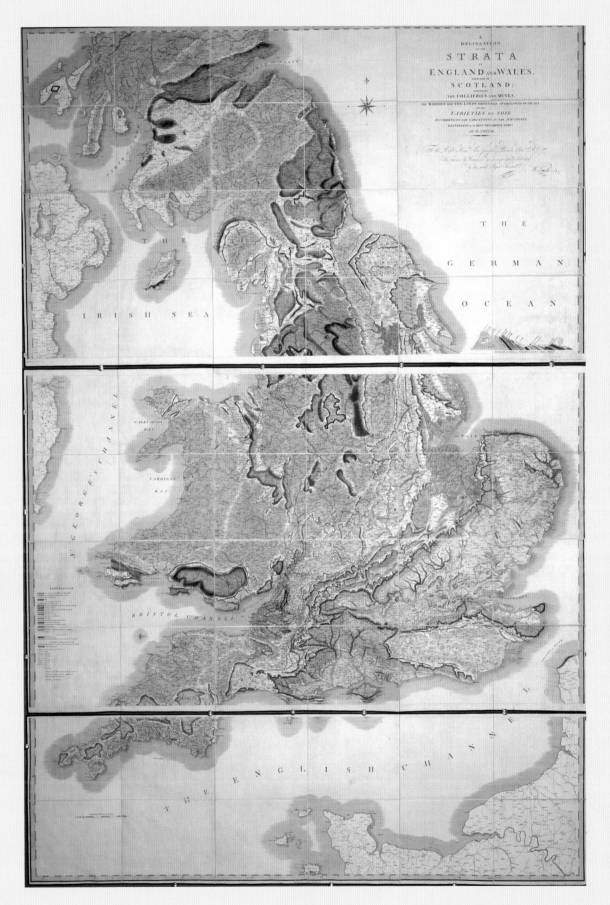

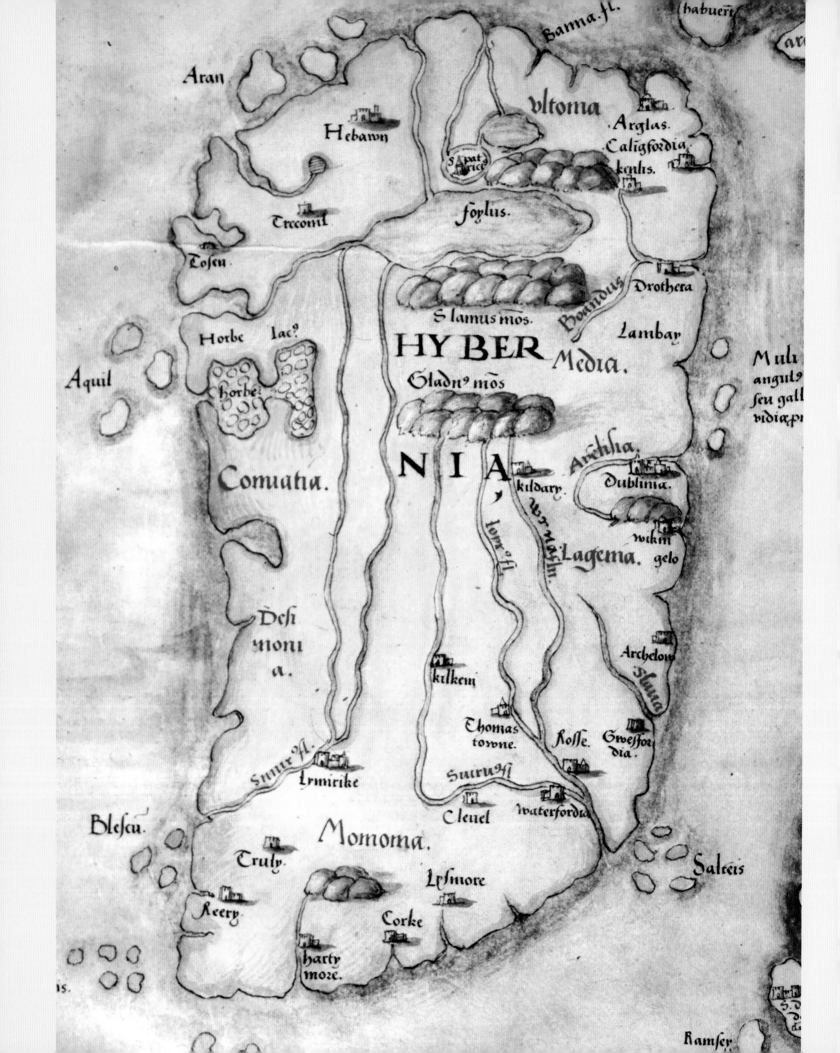

| OPPOSITE | MAP OF HIBERNIA, C. 1534 | This very early map of Ireland follows the custom of the time to use Latin names. (By permission of the British Library: Cotton Augustus I.i.9)

Kingdom, was formally united with England in 1801, but Eire was established as the Irish Free State in 1922.

Other sizeable islands included within the United Kingdom are the Isle of Wight off the south coast of England and Anglesey off the north-west coast of Wales, along with the Scillies archipelago – the first landfall that is sighted from an Atlantic crossing – to the south-west, and the Orkneys, Shetlands and Hebridean archipelagos to the north and north-west of Scotland. In demonstration of the quirkiness of the United Kingdom's history, both the Isle of Man in the Irish Sea and the Channel Islands group are not a part of it, but are direct dependencies of the British Crown with external affairs and defence administered through a governor.

From a maritime surveying viewpoint the coastline is highly indented with over 12,000 miles of coastline and its charting has always represented a challenge. It could be said that the British have salt water in their blood as no point is more than 75 miles from the sea. The main island of Great Britain is the world's eighth largest with an area of 84,549 square miles. Its greatest length is 605 miles and at its widest is 330 miles between the coasts of Pembrokeshire and Norfolk.

Whilst tectonic shift is now relatively minimal at about 1 centimetre a year, the British Isles themselves are tilting at the rate of about 2 millimetres a year. Released from the weight of the ice sheet from the last Ice Age, the north-western shores are rising, while the south-eastern coasts are sinking. Glacial action also acted to pummel and score the lakes and lochs of Cumbria and Scotland, the loughs of Northern Ireland, the valleys of Wales, and created the innumerable inlets that man has been able to turn to his advantage as harbours and ports. Britain's coastline is subjected to the tides and currents of four different seas – the Atlantic, the Irish Sea, the North Sea and the English Channel, the waters of which funnel and eddy around the smaller islands and off-shore obstacles. The warming temperate influence of the Gulf Stream also magnifies the moon's tidal effect, strengthening the scouring seas along the western coastline.

ROCKS AND HAZARDS

A glance at an atlas, or its maritime equivalent, a neptune, can concentrate the mind on the dangers of these seas. Some prominent points of these Isles have earned their names through respect for the awesome power of nature that reminds us, no matter how advanced our technology, that the seaman is still a guest on the sea, and tragedy awaits the unwary and unprepared. Cape Wrath, off the north-west tip of Scotland, Bloody Foreland off Donegal in Ireland, and the ironic name for the prodigious overfalls in the Pentland Firth, off Scotland's north-east coast, marked on Admiralty charts as 'The Merry Men of May', are but a few. Even a visitor from North America is not immune. The Canadian aircraft carrier Bonaventure, a large ship exercising with the British Navy in the 1960s lost three precious aircraft strapped to her flight deck when she turned into the tide and wind in the Pentland Firth and her 'round-down' on the bow dropped into a wave hole from which she only recovered with difficulty. Other dangerous focal points around our shores sound benign, such as Portland Bill, St Catherine's Point, and the Bell Rock and Eddystone Rock, the two most dangerous rocks in British coastal waters.

By the 1800s the UK Hydrographic Office was making it a priority to search out and chart navigational dangers and, in particular, unsubstantiated reports of rocks or shoals known as vigias. As Hydrographer Captain Thomas Hurd stated in his annual report of 1814: 'An examination or search after the several Islands and Vigias marked in all the old charts of the North and South Atlantic Oceans, but whose reality or existence have long been doubted, would be a very desirable object'. Some 2000 vigias existed on old charts and maps and needed to be determined, and if imaginary, deleted. To find a vigia, as the Admiralty Manual of Hydrographic Surveying states, 'may occupy a considerable time, as experience shows that many reports are based on erroneous observations or deductions'.

Even by 1890 the annual report detailed a new danger off Anglesey, along with the discovery of the Warden Bank in the Clyde, but, more pertinently, it summed up the number of vigias reported that year 'of the most formidable danger' as 75, along with four sandbanks, and 19 reported of necessity because the vessel struck them. In the 1892 report, decent surveys became more urgent as 'the general employment of steam encourages ships to enter narrow waters formerly inaccessible when the motive power was wind. Rocks are discovered in such places even when the survey has been apparently of sufficient completeness'. And in 1895 the annual report said that 'the increasing traffic caused by the expansion of trade, in waters where but a few years ago hardly a vessel was to be met, demands in many cases detailed surveys on a large scale'.

Considerable effort was spent searching for reported hazards that didn't actually exist, such as Aitken's Rock. Hurd's successor, William Parry, had despatched HMS Gannet in 1824, and HMS Harrier and Badger in 1827, and Sir Francis Beaufort, who inherited the anxiety when he took over as Hydrographer

South ELEVATION of the STONE LIGHTHOUSE *completed upon the* EDYSTONE *in 1759.*
Shewing the Prospect of the nearest Land, as it appears from the Rocks in a clear calm Day.

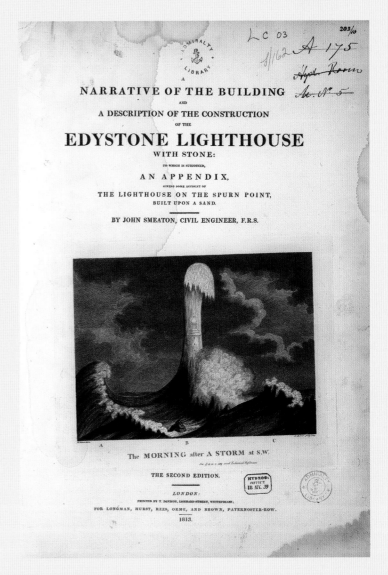

| **ABOVE** | **THE EDDYSTONE LIGHT** | The Eddystone Light is probably the most famous lighthouse in the world, and is built on treacherous rocks 14 miles south-south-west of Plymouth. The engraving shows John Smeaton's construction, the fourth of five lighthouses to be erected. It was completed in 1759 of Cornish granite cut with dove-tailed joints and using a form of quick-drying cement, a formidable construction exercise which required special lifting gear. It lasted for 120 years when, after cracks were discovered, it was removed and reconstructed where it now stands on Plymouth Hoe.

| OPPOSITE | TIDAL MAP OF ENGLAND BY JOHN MARSHALL, C. 1579 | This tidal map of England, whilst naively charming from our perspective, could only have hinted at best as to the tidal streams around the coast. (By permission of the British Library: ROYAL 17.A.II)

The first lighthouse, built by Henry Winstanley in 1698, was of wood in an octagonal shape, and strengthened in 1699. Winstanley was captured by a French privateer during construction, but Louis XIV ordered his release pronouncing that, 'We are at war with England, and not humanity'. Winstanley rebuilt the lighthouse in 1703, testing providence – and losing – as he wanted to sit out a storm in the lighthouse. The storm that came was one of the worst ever recorded and when it abated both he and the lighthouse were gone.(UKHO © British Crown Copyright)

in 1829, sent HMS *Pylades* and HMS *Despatch*, but all were unable to find even a bank of submerged seaweed to explain at least seven reports on earlier charts in a mean position of 55° 16' N, 11° 40' W, 70 miles north-west of 'Urris' (Erris) Head on the north-west coast of Ireland, which, with its reported 4 feet protruding above the water, represented a significant hazard for ships sailing around the north of Scotland and heading towards the Newfoundland cod banks. Finally, in 1830 Beaufort put two 10-gun brigs, the Onyx (Lieutenant Dawson) and the Leverat (Lieutenant Worth) under the command of Captain (later Vice-Admiral) Alexander Vidal, well-known for his east and west African coastal surveys. The search took from 6 June to 31 August, checking every reported position, trawling throughout the area encompassed by them, yet finding nothing.

The reverse scenario held when locals were oblivious to the presence of dangerous rocks. In 1891 HMS *Knight Errant*, while

| CHART OF THE SOUTH WESTERN APPROACHES BY WILLIAM HEATHER, 1797 |

The 'recommended' sailing route from the Atlantic to London is shown on this chart as 'The Fair Way' and marked by sailing ships. It must have been some comfort to know that, in the event of disaster out at sea, other ships were likely to be sailing nearby, although at night lights needed to be burnt at the masthead and astern. The international rules for avoiding collision at sea developed from custom and etiquette and were first incorporated into International Law in 1910, then re-written and agreed in 1948. They stipulate the avoiding action to be taken if vessels are on a collision bearing and the lights that have to be shown, port and starboard navigation lights, and white steaming lights aloft, the number and positioning depending on the vessel's size. Also in force today are channel separation regulations, as the English Channel is arguably the busiest in the world. (Admiralty Library Manuscript Collection: Vz 2/1)

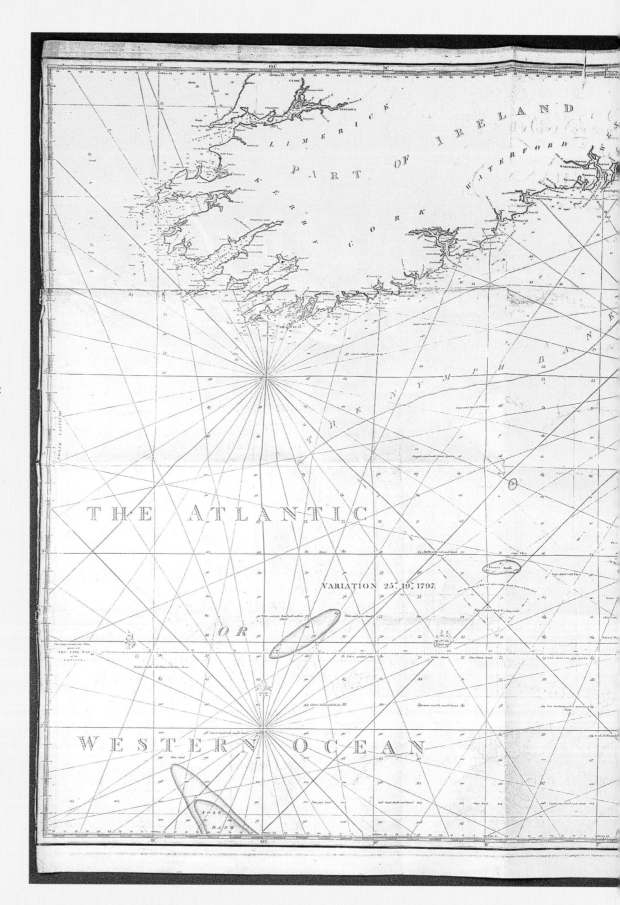

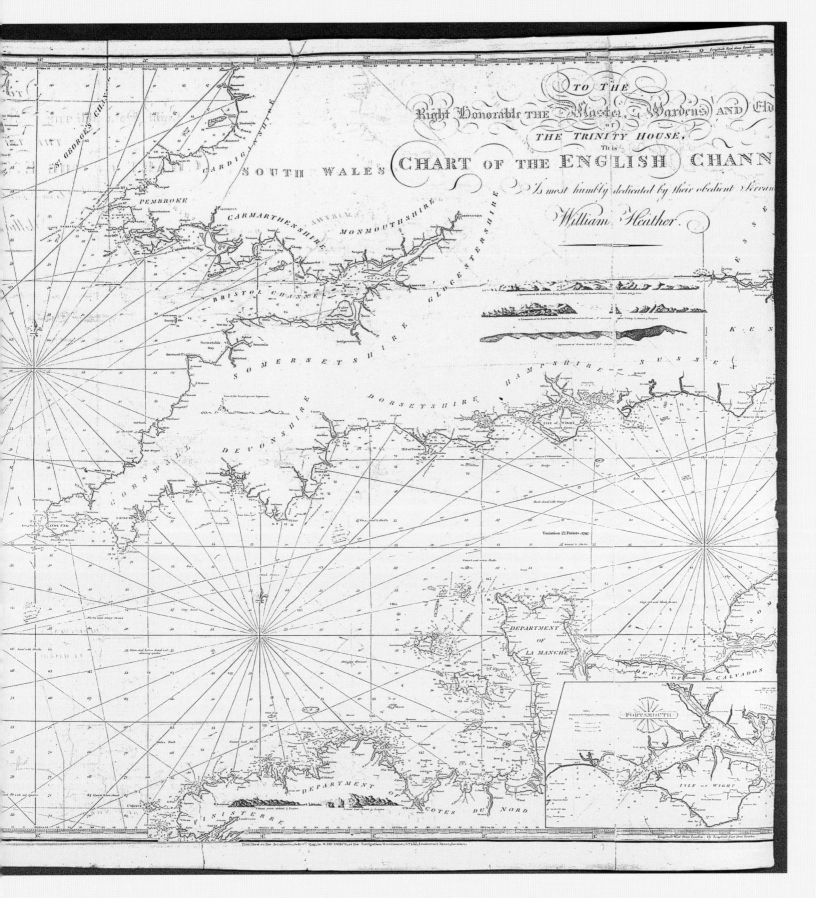

surveying a large-scale chart of the anchorage of Lamlash (in the Scottish Isle of Arran, along the Firth of Clyde) as a safe anchorage for squadrons of battleships, found a pinnacle of rock unknown to local fishermen.

Shoals would not present a problem if they remained immutable, but they don't. Many are found in the North Sea or English Channel, for example the Goodwin Sands and the shoals off the Norfolk Coast. Formed by the inundation of an extensive area of the continental crust, the North Sea is still subsiding and the featureless bottom topography conceals a deep sedimentary basin with over 20,000 feet of sediment deposited over the last 250 million years. In the Norwegian trough are contained most of the North Sea Oil and gas deposits. The banks of the North Sea, the Dogger, Fisher and Jutland Banks, are actually glacial moraines. These sediments are constantly being carried along and deposited by the tidal currents, particularly so where there is enough sea-room for large waves to develop, and the Thames Estuary and the Wash are two of the many prone areas.

Continuous surveying is needed to monitor the more notorious shoals, inevitably those by shipping lanes, and dredging to maintain the depth of water. In 1888, HMS Triton was under the command of Captain Tizard during survey work in the Thames Estuary. He re-sounded the Duke of Edinburgh (called the Edinburgh Channel today), Alexandra, Prince's and Knob Channels to find that the central patch in the first channel had shoaled to 22 feet. In 1892 Triton, now under the command of Captain Maxwell, surveyed the Duke of Edinburgh Channel again and found decreased depths sufficiently worrying to report back, 'whether the channel will be finally reclosed, or whether the shoal will be arrested in its concretion, time only can show'. This was the main channel to the port of London. By 1896 Triton was checking the Goodwin Sands and 'found considerable changes since the 1887 survey'. And in 1901, Triton, this time commanded by Captain G E Richards, found important shoaling off the North Foreland with a steady increase on the Shingles Patch.

The violence of an enemy's navy is little compared to that of the sea, and has accounted for, roughly, only one in eight of the 11,000 or so shipwrecks resting on the continental shelf around the British Isles. This is an approximate figure, and the Wrecks Section of the UKHO, who produce the wreck charts, are the first to admit that they cannot know them all. Reports are often inexact and, even with today's sonar technology and microwave radio ranging, no more than 65 per cent of the sea bed has been scanned. But the position of underwater obstructions, which include oil and gas pipes and telecommunication cables, is important to all shipping, whether naval or commerical, and the UKHO, as the primary chart agency, compiles the information

from many sources. The Government-run Maritime Coastguard Agency (MCA) prioritises surveys between the different 'user' needs and each of the main port authorities such as London, Liverpool, Avonmouth and Milford Haven have their own Port Surveyors to keep the channels clear.

The MCA's main role is the coordination of search and rescue for any sea emergency, from a drowning swimmer to a collision of supertankers, from a rambler fallen from a cliff to an injured yachtsman or a burning oil rig. It constantly monitors the sea coast and will alert and summon the best response to effect a rescue, be it the local lifeboat, Navy or RAF helicopter, cliff rescuers or inshore lifeboats.

One of the most important organisations for lifesaving is the Royal National Lifeboat Institution (RNLI). Set up in 1824, it operates as a registered charity reliant on public contributions to fund an active lifeboat fleet of 332 boats at 233 lifeboat stations situated strategically around the coast. It performs magnificent work. For example, in 2004, in 7656 lifeboat, inshore lifeboat and rescue water craft launches, 433 lives were saved and 7507 people rescued. Progressive in outlook, the RNLI has introduced four hovercraft lifeboats for rescue on mudflats and tidal estuaries, where conventional boats can't reach, such as Morecambe Bay, Hunstanton and Southend-on-sea.

TRINITY HOUSE

The origins of Trinity House date back to a charitable guild of sea samaritans established by Archbishop Stephen Langton in the twelfth century, although the first official record is the grant of a Royal Charter by Henry VIII in 1514 to a fraternity of mariners called the Guild of the Holy Trinity, 'so that they might regulate the pilotage of ships in the King's streams'. In 1604 James I conferred on Trinity House rights concerning compulsory pilotage of shipping and the exclusive right to license pilots in the River Thames. Trinity House was the Pilotage Authority for London and over 40 other districts, including the major ports of Southampton and Harwich, until responsibility for District Pilotage was transferred to Port and Harbour Authorities under the 1987 Pilotage Act.

Today the Corporation is comprised of a fraternity of approximately 300 brethren drawn from the Royal and Merchant Navies and leading figures in the shipping industry. Its Master since 1969 has been the Duke of Edinburgh. A similar service is provided in Scotland and the Isle of Man by the Northern Lighthouse Board.

As a landsman refers to a landmark, so a seamen refers to a sea-mark, which is the generic term used for any prominent floating

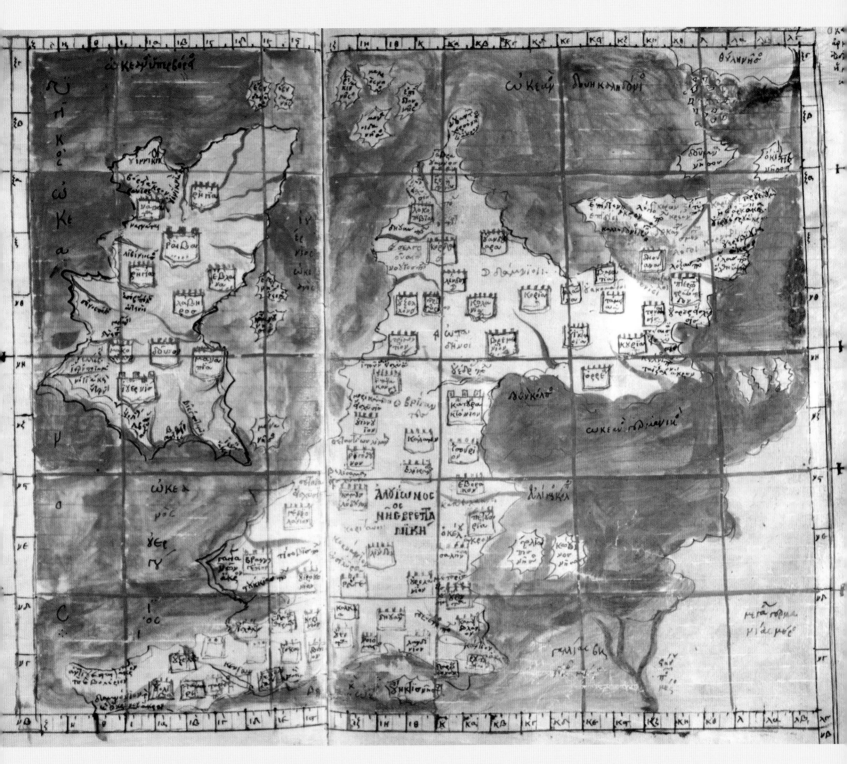

| MAP OF THE WHOLE BRITISH ISLES AFTER PTOLEMY,
FOURTEENTH CENTURY | Claudius Ptolemaeus, probably a Greek, was
born in Egypt and worked for most of his life in Alexandria. He was an astronomer
nd mathematician who laid down the foundations of cartography, inventing, around
AD 150, a number of projections to represent the Earth's curved surface on a flat
surface. Ptolemy's great work, Geographia, was lost with the fall of the Roman
Empire and only came to light in the fourteenth century when the Greek version
surfaced in Constantinople. The map shown here, which is based on his
calculations, comes from the Greek monastery of Vatopedi, Mount Athos, and
is one of the earliest known renderings of the British Isles. With place names in
Greek and a grid latitude and longitude system, the monks' understanding of the
position of the British Isles off Europe and their shape would have been compiled
from the reports of Mediterranean traders. (By permission of the British Library:
ADD.1939)

navigational mark such as a buoy or lightship. A landmark to a seaman is any fixed point on land that can be used to obtain a compass bearing or as a leading mark to indicate a safe channel (early examples can be seen on the charts of Greenvile Collins, see later). Confusingly, in the early days of navigation, marks set up specifically on shore were called sea-marks and Trinity House, in its charter, was empowered by Elizabeth I to set these up where necessary as an aid to navigation. Anyone found interfering or destroying them could be fined £100, or outlawed if unable to pay, since 'by the destroying and taking away of certain steeples, woods, and other marks standing upon the main shores…being as beacons and marks of ancient time, divers ships have been miscarried, perished, and lost in the sea'.

Buoys were first set to mark navigational channels, spoil ground, and banks in European waters in the late fifteenth century. Trinity House laid the first in the River Thames in 1538; buoys to mark the entrances of principal harbours and ports followed soon afterwards; then rocks and shoals were marked around the coast. In the beginning a buoy was a balk of timber with a staff positioned on top. An improvement was similar to a beer keg, then, as iron ships were launched, buoys were made of metal too. Through tradition four distinct shapes developed – can, conical, spherical or spar – whilst mooring buoys for ships are generally cylindrical.

The largest form of sea-mark is the lightship. These are moored fore and aft, and have a powerful light, rather as a floating lighthouse. They are usually a 'dumb vessel', that is with no propulsion, and are used where a lighthouse is impracticable, typically over a shoal or sandbank such as Smith's Knoll in the North Sea. They are painted red with their name writ large along the ship's side. One of the most well known was the South Goodwin light vessel when she tragically became the first Trinity lightship to be wrecked on 27 November 1954. In winds of over 80 knots she broke from her two huge sea anchors and was blown on to the very sandbank she was warning against, with only one survivor from the crew. Many lightships are being replaced by large buoys known as Lanbys, around 12 metres in diameter and with a lattice mast some 12 metres above sea level, a 16-mile range light and powerful foghorn and radar beacon, in depths of up to 300 feet.

The first lighthouse built by Trinity House was at Lowestoft in 1609, which was part of a series of lights to help guide vessels through a maze of sandbanks between Happisburgh in Norfolk and Lowestoft in Suffolk. The lighthouses were paid for by a levy charged on vessels leaving the ports of Newcastle, Hull, Boston and King's Lynn, a method of payment which is similar to the current light dues system that remains in use today.

The next 200 years saw a proliferation of lighthouses, many privately owned, with an annual fee paid either to the Crown or Trinity House. The owners of the private lights were allowed to levy light dues from passing ships when they reached port. Many of the private lights were unreliable and in 1836 legislation was passed for the compulsory purchase of all private lights in England, Wales and the Channel Islands and bring them under the management of Trinity House. The previous owners were compensated on the basis of their receipts from light dues, and the highest payment of nearly half a million pounds in respect of Skerries Lighthouse, off Anglesey, was paid.

EARLY CHARTMAKING

One of the very earliest mentions of England comes through a Greek navigator Pytheas, who lived in the Greek colony of Massilia (Marseilles today) and was a contemporary of Alexander the Great, so placing him in the fourth century BC. Although his original writings are lost, we know from various references that he sailed on a long voyage to northern Europe, sailing along the east coast of Britain as far north as the Orkneys and Shetlands, which he called Thule. Pytheas was a skilled astronomer as well as navigator, and was one of the first to use the altitude of the sun to fix the latitude of places – he fixed Marseilles remarkably accurately, which Ptolemy used for his renowned map of the Mediterranean. He was also one of the first to ascertain that the moon caused the periodical fluctuations of the tides.

Portolani or books of sailing directions, known in England as rutters of the sea, existed in medieval times, before the chart as we have come to know it was conceived. One of the earliest mentions is in Adam of Bremen's *Ecclesiastical History* in the twelfth century, which summarises an earlier document that briefly sets out the stages of a voyage (crusade) from Maas to Acre in Palestine with a distance from point to point by the number of days' sailing and a rough direction. The only point given on the English coast is Pral, which is perhaps Prawle Point or Portland Bill. As navigation during the Middle Ages had not progressed beyond 'caping' (keeping to the coastline and sailing from cape to cape), rutters were essentially a record of the land seen from seaward, and would contain sailing directions and features between the maximum distance a cape could be seen – about a kenning (20 miles).

Probably the earliest known original English rutter is held among the Marquess of Salisbury's family archives at Hatfield House in Hertfordshire. In 1537 Henry VIII's third wife, Jane Seymour, had died giving birth to his only legitimate son. Henry needed another wife to guarantee the male lineage and his

| MARITIME MAP OF THE BRITISH ISLES AT THE TIME OF THE
SPANISH ARMADA BY ROBERT ADAMS, 1588 | This maritime map
has the track of the broken Spanish Armada blown by the 'Protestant Wind'
to the north of Scotland and into the Atlantic. It gives a clear picture of
Elizabethan England and the British Isles in relation to Europe in 1588.
(By permission of the British Library: MAPS.C.3.66.5)

Chief Minister, Thomas Cromwell, found a politically expedient
marriage prospect in Anne of Cleves. However, with the political
risks prevailing in Europe after Henry's ecclesiastical break with
the Papacy and his unpopularity with the Holy Roman Emperor,
it was felt that Anne should be brought from Holland to England
by sea in the company of Henry's royal fleet.

The parlous state of English cartography was emphasised
when no charts or rutters to guide the fleet could be found and
two experienced sailing masters, Richard Couche from Dover
and John Aborough from Devon, were instructed to secretly
check out the route from the Zuider Zee to Dover. The only book
of sailing directions printed in English at that time, entitled The
Rutter of the Sea, was a guide to the English Channel, although
covering voyages to Bordeaux and Andalusia. The Dutch pilot
book published in 1532 by Jan Seuerszoon as the Kaert van der
Zee was too parochial.

In the event Anne was brought overland to Calais to make
the short crossing, but the resulting rutter gives a clear idea of

what must have been one of thousands of rolls of sailing directions
laboriously copied by hand, jealously guarded by their navigating
owners and perhaps handed down within the family during the
Middle Ages and into the sixteenth century, as they were known
to be used long after the first English printed pilot in 1523. The
Hatfield House rutter consists of four narrow rolls of parchment
sewn together end to end, which gives an unrolled size 3½ feet
long by 6 inches wide. That it survives is only because it was
never actually used at sea, and we must assume that these items
would have been thrown overboard once worn out with use and
sea water contamination. From the detailed directions on it we
know the general form that the Tudor rutter took, which was that

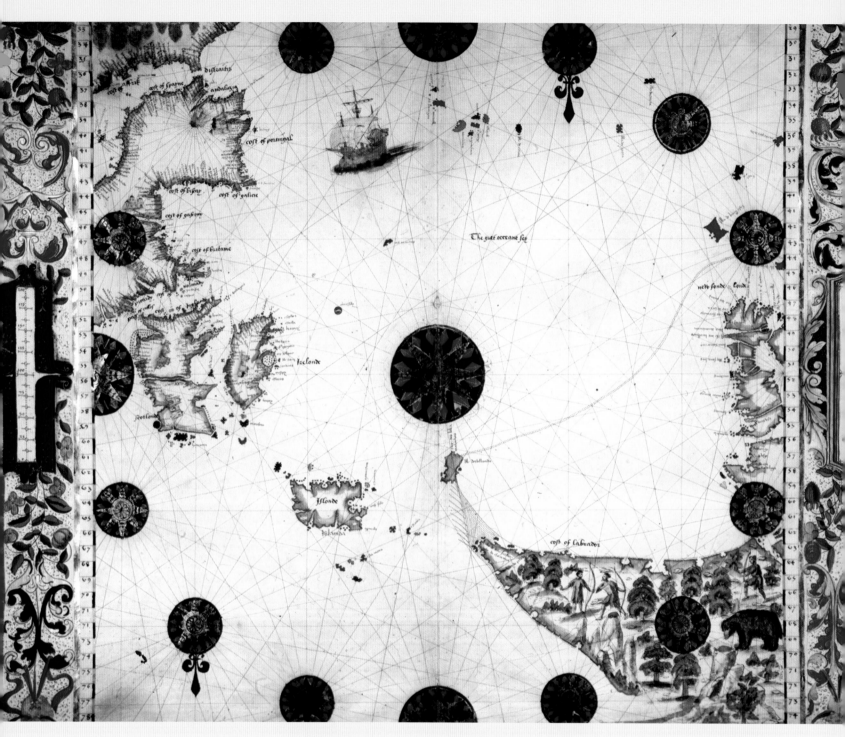

| CHART OF THE NORTH ATLANTIC BY JEAN ROTZ, 1542 | As one of the leading cartographers of his day, Jean Rotz was respected for the accuracy and care of his charts, which lead to his appointment as Hydrographer to Henry VIII, and then to Henri II of France. One of his cartographical characteristics was always to orientate South to the top of the page, and to construct, often from his own observations, his charts with the portolan format. This chart shows the British Isles as they were understood in 1542 with Scotland an island and the coast of Labrador and North America generously extended towards Europe, with Newfoundland adjacent and Iceland between. (By permission of the British Library: ff.21v–22)

of a progressive description with the next land or sea mark only identifiable or attainable from the current one.

Further evidence of the lack of available navigational information at this time is shown by the petitioning of leading sailing masters to Henry to create an organisation to control pilotage on the River Thames. Trinity House was granted a charter of incorporation in 1513 to counter the menace of foreign pilots who often knew the approaches to London better than their English counterparts. Even in Elizabethan times, Dr John Dee, the Queen's soothsayer, astronomer and so-called magician, wrote somewhat apprehensively:

> ...by colour and pretence of coming about their feat of fishing, do subtly and secretly use Soundings and Searchings of our Channels, Deeps, Shoals, Banks and Bars along the Sea Coasts, and in our Haven Mouths also, and up in our Creeks, sometimes in our Bays and sometimes in our Roads &c. Taking good Marks, for the avoiding of the dangers: And also trying good Landings. And so making perfect Charts of all our Coasts round about England and Ireland, are become almost perfecter in them than the most part of our Masters, Loadsmen or Pilots are.

The English navigator would rely heavily on the rutter, given the meagre navigation equipment of medieval times, which he used along with the compass, and lead and line for sounding depths. Indeed before the introduction of the compass, the portolan charts bore a wind rose, culminating ultimately in 64 directions, with each of the eight main winds named. This became the design basis for the compass rose for which the Arab sidereal rose arrangement of 32 points of 11½ degrees, drawn out as rhumb lines (from the Spanish rumbos meaning bearings) on charts, was favoured over the Chinese cosmogonic rose of 12 or 24 points. The portolan charts were based on a framework of 16 compass roses equally spaced and arranged in a circle, with radiating rhumb lines that navigators would use as a guide to lay off a course to steer. The English word 'compass' derives from the pair of dividers used as an instrument for drawing the compass rose and for measuring distances on the chart's scale.

The intended invasion of England in 1588 by Philip II with an Armada of 130 ships, transporting an army of 30,000, to dethrone the Protestant Elizabeth and prevent England's support of the Netherland's fight for independence from Spain, provides us with a further insight into the state of English charting by a look at what the Spanish sailing masters took on board.

The first was a copy of *Spiegel der Zeevaerdt* (Mirror of the Sea) by Lucas Janszoon Wagenaer, a Dutch pilot born around

1534 in Enkhuizen (or Enchuysen) on the Zuider Zee. He met the needs of the increase in trade in northern Europe by compiling a collection of charts published in Leiden in 1584, printed by Christopher Plantin. It comprised a manual of navigation, a pilot book and 45 charts of the European coastline as far south as Cadiz, northwards into the North Sea and Baltic, and included the English coast from the Isle of Wight to the Strait of Dover. Greeted with acclaim, it was additionally published in French, German and English editions. In England it was translated by Sir Anthony Ashley and published, with completely re-engraved charts, as *The Mariner's Mirrour*, in the year of the Armada.

In England, the word 'waggoner', a corruption of Wagenaer, came to describe any sea-atlas. Perhaps the best-known British example is the *Waggoner of the Great South Seas*, by William Hack, a sometime buccaneer and member of the Thames School (see later). The waggoners were highly picturesque with complex cartouches, ships and sea-monsters. Cliffs and coastlines were drawn in elevation, information on anchorages, dangerous rocks and symbols were added, which are still in use today. They were the first printed charts to show soundings, measured in fathoms and reduced to mean half-tide values, and a scale in English, Spanish and Dutch leagues. The Spanish also had two manuscript copies by the Portuguese cartographer Luis Teixeria and a chart of the western Europe coastline by Domenico de Vigliarolo (variously Vigliaroula and Domingo Villeroel), a Neapolitan cleric and cartographer in the Casa de Contratacion in Seville, which give a better idea of the outline of the British Isles, particularly of Scotland, than contemporary surviving Portuguese charts show. Philip also possessed Abraham Ortelius's *Theatrum Orbis Terrarum* with reasonable maps of western Europe and the British Isles.

An official set of sailing directions *Derrotero de las costas de Bretaña, Normandia, Picardia, hasta Flandes, y de la de Inglaterra, Manga de Bristol y Sant Iorge, y parte de la costa de Irlanda* was published by Antonio Álvarez in Lisbon on 30 March 1588 on the orders of the inexperienced commander of the Armada, the Duke of Medina Sidonia. There is a copy in the British Library. It was probably compiled from Spanish commercial captains as it contains optimistic advice to pick up a pilot, expected to have Roman Catholic sympathies, at Lundy, Tenby or Caldey before sailing up the Bristol Channel or, if aiming for Dobla (Dover) or Londres (London), from las Dunas (the Downs). It has directions and distances between ports and other important landmarks, tidal flows, shoal positions, sea bottom nature, but no defence information except to point out the chain across Falamua (Falmouth) Harbour, and no information north of Tierra bermeja (The Naze near Harwich) along the east coast or, to the west, north of la Isla de Baldresay (Bardsey Island), Oliet (Holyhead), Ysal de Man in the Irish Sea, Gatafurda (Waterford) on the east coast of Ireland and Drosey (Dursey Island), los Guelmes (the Skelligs) and Sant Michel (Darrynane Harbour). A lesson hard won by many navigators – always to have the next chart beyond your planned destination available on board – was not taken by the Armada which had no intention to sail further north, but was eventually forced to do so in order to evade capture.

Philip's second and third abortive Armadas of 1596 and 1597 sailed with a set of five sketches made by an English Catholic pilot, Nicholas Lambert, which are held in the Museo Naval, Madrid. They are some of the earliest surviving charts of the ports where landings were considered – Milford Haven, Falmouth, Plymouth and Dartmouth – along with an area of the Isle of Wight with Southampton and Portsmouth.

BRITISH CHARTMAKERS

By 1540 Henry VIII, following the lead of his father Henry VII, was building his navy. A Scot, David Ross, had settled in Dieppe, and his son, Jean Rotz, worked as a pilot for the local ship owner, Jean Ango, sailing his ships worldwide from 1530. Rotz compiled a neptune of 11 charts, which covered the known world, including, surprisingly, much of Australia, which he took to the court of Francis II in Paris. Unsuccessful in his bid for the post of Royal Hydrographer, he sailed for London and presented his charts, the 'Boke of Idography', with a compass he had invented and a paper on navigation to Henry VIII. He was appointed Royal Hydrographer, and advised on the charting of England's southern ports and on the expansion of the navy. With Henry's approaching death, Rotz made a deal with France's new king, Henri II, to bring plans of English and Scottish ports, even arranging a fake arrest at sea as cover, in exchange for his return to France and the chance to set up a new life in Dieppe.

Rotz's intelligence probably helped in the ousting of the English from her last French possession, Calais, in 1558. Many of Rotz's charts were compiled using the portolan style, from his own observations, with coastlines, islands rocks and shoals and iconic drawings of the land to typify the peoples and activities there.

While the Dutch lead the world in the production of maps and charts in the sixteenth century, with famous cartographers such as Blaeu, de Wit, Hendrick Doncker, Pieter Goos and, significantly, the Van Keulen family, one Englishman produced beautiful charts that were the first to be based on Mercator's Projection, introduced in 1569. The man was Robert Dudley, the son of a dalliance between Robert Dudley, Earl of Leicester and Lady Douglas Sheffield, the daughter of the Lord High Admiral, the Earl

of Effingham, who settled in Florence and worked for the Grand Duke of Tuscany, Cosimo II. He produced three volumes of charts, all painstakingly prepared, engraved by an Italian, Antonio Lucini, and published in Florence in 1645 and 1646. *Dell' Arcano del Mare* (Secrets of the Sea) contained 130 charts, along with details of all the navigational instruments of the time, examples of shipwork, and a plan for a naval force with five rates of ship.

The breakthrough of Mercator's Projection was that it allowed the curved surface of the Earth to be represented on a flat surface, using a grid system with meridians of longitude crossing parallels of latitude at right angles. Despite its merits, it was very slow to be adopted. Edward Wright, a Fellow of Caius College, Cambridge, realised how important Mercator's solution was, but its application was very much the ambit of academia. In writing *Certaine Errors in Navigation Detected and Corrected*, published in 1599, Wright explained the advantages of Mercator's chart system and how it worked for the average seaman's understanding. He used the simple analogy of a pig's bladder blown up inside a cylinder. Mercator's Projection made it possible for the mariner to plot a single, straight (rhumb) line from one point to another as a course to steer. Earlier charts made no allowance for the Earth's curvature and, as a consequence, the mariner had to constantly correct his course.

The first English attempt to compete with the Dutch in the marketing of sea-atlases or waggoners was John Seller, a cartographer and scientific instrument-maker based in Wapping, where sailors disembarking at the docks often had useful information to sell. He began producing *The English Pilot*, Books I and II of which were published in 1671–2.

The printed chart would eventually supersede the manuscript chart, of course, but what is surprising is how long hand-made charts continued to be in demand and to flourish alongside them. Their advantage lay in their robustness and their personalisation. Hand-drawn 'Plattes' were constructed on vellum, which was tough and resisted salt water. A sea captain could have a chart made to cover the area he needed, bearing in mind that in the sixteenth and seventeenth centuries a ship's position wasn't plotted on a chart; it was used as a visual guide.

A platt-makers' 'school', in the sense of apprentice training rather than of practice and production, grew to meet that demand, dubbed recently The Thames School. They were nearly all, peculiarly, liverymen of the Worshipful Company of Drapers, one of the 12 Great Companies of the City of London, ranked third behind the Mercers and Grocers. It seems that nearly all chartmakers working in England in the seventeenth century were members. The earliest recorded member is a John Walsh in 1554, although no known chart by him exists. But he had a

| TITLE PAGE TO THE *ATLAS MARITIMUS* BY JOHN SELLER, 1698 | Each copy of Seller's *Atlas Maritimus*, which was first published in 1675, was of composite make-up, with the selection of charts chosen by the individual purchaser. The title page shows examples of the cross-staff, used for taking the angles of heavenly bodies; a backstaff, a Gunter Quadrant, for getting the altitude of the stars; globes, a chart and a seventeenth-century compass. (The National Archives {PRO}: FO/925/4111)

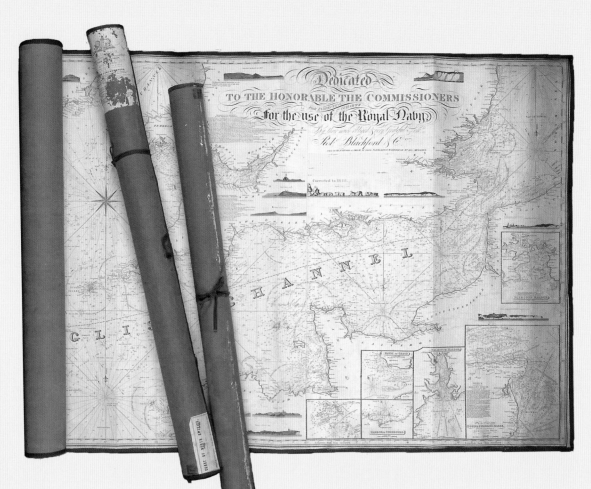

well-known platt-maker of the time, John Daniell, apprenticed to him in 1590. He, in turn, is described in the Drapers' archives as taking on six 'Apprentice Patternmakers' in 1622 at the Irongate, including William Hanman 'seacard drawer at S Katherine by the Tower' and Nicholas Comberford, and so on for seven generations until the 1750s.

Apprenticeship, unique in medieval times as a system to learn a skilled trade, had advantages for both master and apprentice. Boys between the ages of 14 and 18 would be bound to a master, who had a cheap form of assistance while the apprentice had

| ABOVE | CHART OF THE ENGLISH CHANNEL, FIRST PUBLISHED IN 1835 BY ROBERT BLACHFORD & CO. (THIS EXAMPLE PUBLISHED IN 1848 AFTER JAMES IMRAY HAD JOINED WITH BLACHFORD) | This photograph shows how the large Blueback charts produced by commercial chartsellers specifically for the Merchant Service were stored. They were often printed on three sheets joined together and could be as large as 3 feet 6 inches by 6 feet. Blachford's chart portfolio was the strongest of the various chart publishers at the time for the North Sea and Baltic. The origin of 'Blueback' derives from the strong blue paper used as a protective backing to the chart. This example has the typical characteristics of a Blueblack chart with inset harbour plans and navigational views. (By courtesy of Imray, Norie, Laurie and Wilson Ltd)

security for seven years, and became fully qualified in an independent trade.

The school's style was a direct influence from William Borough, sometime Master of Trinity House and Chief Pilot of the Muscovy Company, Elizabeth I's most distinguished hydrographer and an experienced navigator. He was trained by Sebastian Cabot, son of Giovanni Caboto, the Venetian navigator who, in the Mathew, discovered the cod banks off Newfoundland under Henry VII's auspice. The Thames School also took influence from the early Mediterranean portolans using rich colouring in ink and beautiful heraldic cartouches. They were mounted on two oak boards hinged so that they would close together for carrying and protection. The earliest surviving example is one drawn by John Daniell of the South Atlantic in 1614.

The Draper cartographers nearly all worked in Radcliff or Wapping, in seventeenth-century London between the Tower and Stepney. John Burston was apprenticed, as were most, for seven years to Comberford, and was in turn Master to John Thornton from 1656 to 1665. Samuel Pepys records seeing Nicholas Comberford on 22 July 1663: '...by water to Ratcliffe and there to speak to Cumberford, the platt-maker. And there saw his manner of working which is very fine'. Joel Gascoyne

was apprenticed to John Thornton, one of the best-known figures of his time, being appointed Hydrographer to the Hudson Bay Company and to the East India Company. He worked with John Seller, finishing Books III and IV of his *English Pilot*, and Atlas Maritimus (c. 1675). Pepys' career with the navy was long-spanned and in October 1680 he again wrote, 'Get Gascoin the platmaker to compare the original and later Waggoners with Anthony Ashley's and Seller's new maps'.

In the seventeenth century the impunity with which the Dutch had sailed up the Thames Estuary using Dutch charts under Admiral de Ruyter during the Second Anglo-Dutch War (1665–7) and burned naval ships in the River Medway, bombed the Royal Dockyard at Chatham and blockaded London, brought home the need for a set of English coastal charts. The Dutch knew more about our coasts than we did, and further consternation arose when it was realised that a large proportion of charts in John Seller's *The English Pilot* had either been reprinted or copied from old Dutch plates. Samuel Pepys, First Secretary to the Admiralty in 1673, was instrumental in persuading Charles II in 1681 to appoint Captain Greenvile Collins, with the title Hydrographer to the King, to carry out the first real survey of British harbours and coasts. Collins was already recognised as a navigator of ability through his appointment as a Younger Brother of Trinity House. He took command of the Merlin yacht to make a survey of the sea coasts of the Kingdom with just a measuring chain, lead line and compass. He measured the coastline with the chain and took bearings of all the headlands. He measured latitude with a quadrant, but had no way of measuring longitude. The longitude problem would not be solved until John Harrison's chronometer, H4, was recognised and awarded the Longitude Prize almost a century later in 1773.

Starting out from Dover, the daunting and expensive under-taking took seven years to complete and Collins published his results as *Great Britain's Coasting Pilot* in 1693. It comprised 48 charts, 27 pages of tide tables and sailing directions and four pages of coastal views. In the same year the beautifully produced and superior charts of *Le Neptune François* were published in France by Hubert Jaillot and the elder Cassini. Covering from Norway to the Strait of Gibraltar in 29 coastal charts and including depths along suggested coastline routes, ports, sand-banks and rocks, they gave France the cartographic edge over Britain. The French were to maintain their lead in this field with the formation in 1720 of their national hydrographic office, preceding the British by 75 years with the often ironic situation of the Royal Navy giving battle to the French using French charts.

Collins' achievement, however, should not be underestimated. The first edition sold out by 1728, but was reprinted by chartsellers Mount and Page, who sold it with 19 further editions until 1792. His incredible body of work finally replaced the old Dutch waggoners on which the British had relied for too long.

That Collins' *Coasting Pilot* was in common use up to the end of the eighteenth century is underlined by some entries in the Remark Book of HMS *Salisbury*. In 1760 the Admiralty had decided to make it obligatory that observations of coast and ports visited by navy ships should be rendered to them. These included a standard form of columns with headings that showed the seaman's essential priorities when making harbour by requiring entries of 'Place and time when there', 'descriptions for sailing in and out', 'marks for anchoring', 'of wooding and watering', 'Provisions and refreshments', 'Descriptions of fortifications and landing places', and 'Descriptions in regard to Trade and Shipping'. The entry under 'descriptions for sailing in and out of ports &c' by *Salisbury*'s Captain, Andrew Barkley, and Master, James Robertson, for 1 December 1771 reads, 'see Collins Coasting Pilot', and this is repeated for other dates.

Early in the eighteenth century local pilots began to show remarkable knowledge and charting skill. Piercy Brett's chart of Kent and Sussex (1759), John Scott's of the Humber (1734) and Philip Saumarez' survey of the Channel Islands (1724) belong to this period and Collins' work would have inspired a Welsh sailing master, Lewis Morris, who published a series of charts and plans of harbours, bars, bays and roads of St George's Channel and the Pembrokeshire coast in 1748. These were revised and re-issued by his son, William Morris, in 1801.

But the most important development in British surveying in the eighteenth century came about in the work of Professor

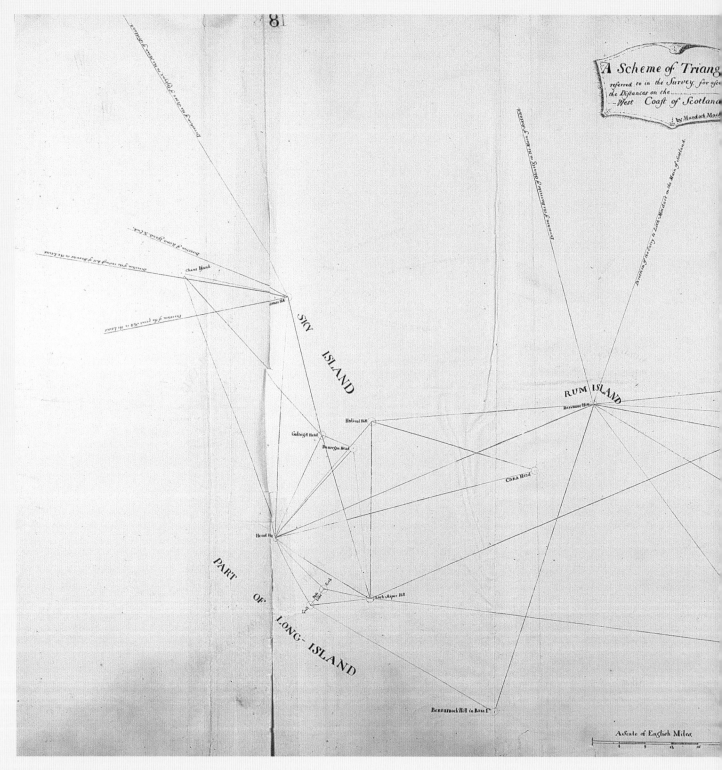

| **PROFESSOR MURDOCH MACKENZIE'S 'SCHEME OF TRIANGLES' FOR MEASURING DISTANCES ON THE WEST COAST OF SCOTLAND, C. 1745** | This is one of Mackenzie's original manuscript charts, held in the Admiralty Library, Portsmouth, showing the 'scheme of triangles' – triangulation – he devised to ascertain distances using landmarks visible from the sea, in this case the islands of Skye, Mull, Rum and Jura. (Admiralty Library Manuscript Collection: Vz 11/49)

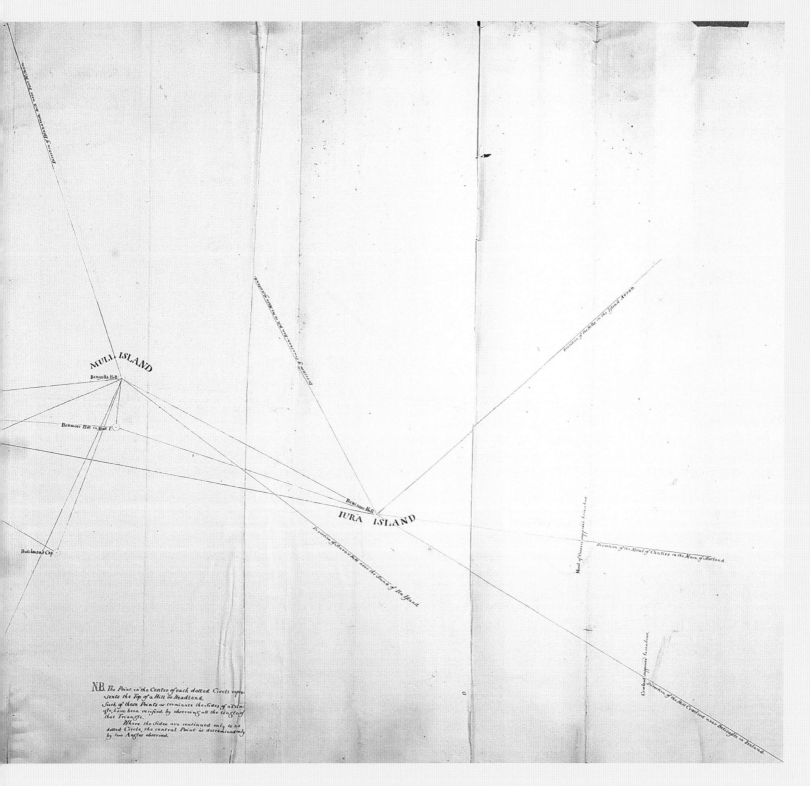

MULL ISLAND

Benvalla Hill

Benmore Hill in Mull I.

Dutchmans Cap

Benmore Hill

IURA ISLAND

NB. The Point in the Center of each dotted Circle repre-
sents the Top of a Hill or Headland.
Such of these Points as terminate the sides of a Triangle, have been verified by observing all the Angles of
that Triangle.
Where the Sides are continued only to the
dotted Circle, the central Point is determined only
by two Angles observed.

Murdock Mackenzie. Towards the mid 1700s the Laird of the Orkneys, James Douglas Earl of Morton, decided to take action to try to reduce the number of shipwrecks around his isles even though he and the islanders were entitled to a share of any salvage. The wrecking of the Swedish East India Company vessel *Svecia* in 1740 on an outlying reef catalysed him into approaching Colin Maclaurin, Mathematics Professor at Edinburgh University, to see if he knew of anyone who could carry out such a survey. Murdoch Mackenzie, a former student and from an Orcadian family, came to mind. Mackenzie raised the money needed – he estimated £638 10s 0d – through subscriptions from foreign East India companies, insurance companies and trading houses, approaching institutions that could benefit from such a survey.

Maclaurin knew Jacques Cassini, one of the four generations of Cassinis who ran the Paris Observatory. He was using a triangulation method to check the land coordinates of France and Mackenzie adapted this system to control his hydrographic survey with a shore-based triangulation network; a maritime surveying breakthrough.

Mackenzie started on the island of Pomona, the main island in the Orkneys, and measuring a base line 3½ miles long on the frozen Loch of Stenness to the north of the island he took theodolite angles from each end of the various beacons he had set up on the surrounding peaks. With the positions of the triangulation stations laid down, he intersected prominent features along the coast as points from which he could then take the angles of boats anchored by significant rocks or reefs, and so plot the position of these dangers and the coastline. From a boat he then took soundings and fixed these by bearings from an azimuth compass. Finally, he checked the scale of his survey by observing latitude by meridian altitude of the sun with Rowley's quadrant on North Ronaldsay and at Kirkwall. He built up a series of five complete charts, had them engraved by Emanuel Bowen in London, and published them in 1750 as a neptune entitled Orcades. The Navy Board had merely loaned him a chain, plane table and theodolite, but now obviously impressed with his work, commissioned him to survey the west coast of Britain and the whole coast of Ireland. By 1770 he had completed Ireland and the British coast south to Pembroke, before he retired. He published a book of his experiences in 1774 entitled Treatise on Maritim Surveying in which he described a new method of plotting a position of a ship on a chart by the 'resection' method, which would use three fixed marks onshore, and a 'station pointer' to the scale of the chart with the end of each of its three legs positioned on the point and at the angle they have been measured. The centre of the station pointer is the position of the ship.

The Admiralty appointed Murdoch Mackenzie's nephew, a lieutenant in the navy of the same name, who had sailed with John Byron in HMS Dolphin in his circumnavigation of 1764–6, to continue where his uncle had left off, surveying down the Bristol Channel to Land's End and then east to Plymouth. The Thames needed attention in 1775 and the Admiralty ordered Mackenzie, who by then was assisted by his cousin, Graeme Spence, to survey the Estuary, and their first chart was of Margate. For this they must have used the resection method Professor Mackenzie had written about and even a form of station pointer, to judge by the abundance of soundings and the clarity of the positions of sandbanks they managed to include. Spence retired in 1803, writing up his sailing directions as Head Maritime Surveyor to the Admiralty until 1811. In 1806 he had shown Captain Thomas Hurd at the Hydrographic Office the station pointer he invented. Hurd asked for one from the First Secretary, William Marsden, which was ordered up from the instrument makers, Edward Troughton. This instrument was used throughout the surveying world for the next 130 years and its impact in allowing a moving vessel to accurately plot resection fixes on board a moving ship is of similar importance to the introduction of echo sounders and electronic navigators such as Decca and Loran.

THE VICTORIAN SURVEY OF BRITISH HOME WATERS

The UK Hydrographic Office was formed by an Order in Council of George III in 1795 (known as the Hydrographical Office until 1839 and today abbreviated to the UKHO). From then on the responsibility for the production and printing of charts fell to the Royal Navy. The groundwork laid down by the first British Hydrographer, Alexander Dalrymple, was followed by Captain Thomas Hurd's determined efforts to get charts out to the fleet and to get the Admiralty to pay a reasonable wage to its employees, by-passing the odious First Secretary to the Admiralty, John Croker, who kept vetoing expansion plans, by selling the charts produced from the navy's own surveyors commercially through appointed Agents.

The extended peace of the nineteenth century seemed to be the occasion to make progress in hydrography and the Hydrographic Office took upon itself the task of charting all the coastlines of the world.

When Admiral Sir Francis Beaufort took over from the Arctic explorer Captain W Parry in 1829, aged 55, he put into action his concept of a 'Grand Survey of the British Isles'. There is a proverb that goes: 'he that would go to sea for pleasure, would go

| ROYAL NAVY SURVEY SHIP, 1902 | An early steam-driven survey vessel is flying her 'paying-off' pennant as she finishes a long hard commission in British waters. Painted by one of her surveyors, he has included white cliffs in the background and we can surmise that she was making for Portsmouth against a prevailing south-westerly with the white cliffs of Dover to starboard. (UKHO © British Crown Copyright)

to hell for a pastime'. This complex and demanding undertaking involved the work of a small, dedicated team of professional, highly competent and tough naval surveyors who worked for years in atrocious weather and often with lousy equipment.

Some died in the service. Captain William Hewett surveyed the whole of the southern section of the North Sea, from Dover to Calais and Orfordness to Scheveningen, by the Dutch coast, including the difficult Dogger Bank, between 1831 and 1840 in HMS Fairy. Albeit he used the earlier surveys of the notable French surveyor, Charles Beautemps-Beaupré, well known for his Australian and Pacific surveys, and those of the Dutchman

Ryk as a basis along the Dutch coast, but it was a formidable undertaking and Hewett didn't survive to see his finished chart. The North Sea is relatively shallow, and vicious steep waves, short from crest to crest quickly build up when the tide is against the wind. The Fairy was caught off Lowestoft in the great storm of 13 and 14 November 1840 and tragically sank with all hands. Even Admiral Sir Edward Belcher, whose intolerance for inefficiency led to multiple officer changes in his ships and courts-martial, wrote to Beaufort of Hewett: 'he will not be replaced by any of the feather-bed crew about Charing Cross…you will not get one to stand the North Sea as he did'.

Commander Michael Slater, who had learned his craft in the Mediterranean under Admiral William Henry Smyth, from 1829 to 1842 surveyed the north-east coast of England and southern Scotland. He followed this with a survey from the River Tay to Thurso Bay, but while he was setting up a shore-side theodolite station there, tragically fell from the cliff to his death.

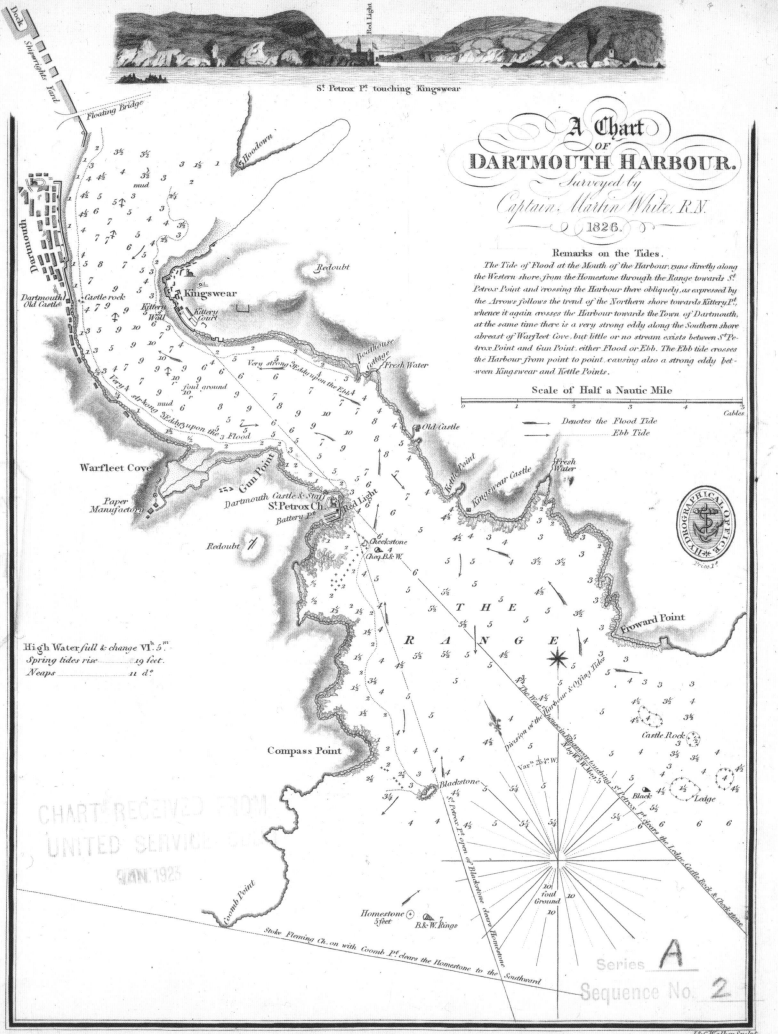

St. Petrox Pt. touching Kingswear

A Chart
OF
DARTMOUTH HARBOUR.
Surveyed by
Captain Martin White, R.N.
1826.

Remarks on the Tides.

The Tide of Flood at the Mouth of the Harbour, runs directly along the Western shore, from the Homestone through the Range towards St. Petrox Point and crossing the Harbour there obliquely, as expressed by the Arrows follows the trend of the Northern shore towards Kittery Pt., whence it again crosses the Harbour towards the Town of Dartmouth, at the same time there is a very strong eddy along the Southern shore abreast of Warfleet Cove, but little or no stream exists between St. Petrox Point and Gun Point, either Flood or Ebb. The Ebb tide crosses the Harbour from point to point, causing also a strong eddy between Kingswear and Kettle Points.

Scale of Half a Nautic Mile

→ Denotes the Flood Tide
→ Ebb Tide

Dartmouth

Floating Bridge

Dock Shipwrights Yard

Hoodown

mud

Redoubt

Kingswear

Kittery Well
Kittery Court

Dartmouth Old Castle
Castle rock

Boathouse Cottage
Fresh Water

Very strong Eddy upon the Ebb

foul ground

Very strong Eddy upon the

Warfleet Cove

Paper Manufactory

Gun Point

Dartmouth Castle & Staff
St. Petrox Ch.
Battery Pt. Red Light

Redoubt

Old Castle

Kettle Point

Kingswear Castle
Fresh Water

Cheekstone
Cheq. B. & W.

THE RANGE

Froward Point

High Water full & change VI h. 5 m.
Spring tides rise _____ 19 feet.
Neaps _____ 11 do.

Compass Point

Castle Rock

Black
Ledge

Blackstone

Division of the Homes in Harbour touching St. Petrox & Offing Tides

Var. 25.4 W.

St. Petrox Pt. open or Blackstone clears Homestone

St. Petrox Pt. clears the Ledge, Castle Rock & Cheekstone

Coomb Point

foul Ground

Homestone 5 feet
B. & W. Rings

Stoke Fleming Ch. on with Coomb Pt. clears the Homestone to the Southward

London Published according to Act of Parliament at the Hydrographical Office of the Admiralty 22nd March 1829

J. & C. Walker Sculpt.

| OPPOSITE | CHART OF DARTMOUTH HARBOUR BY CAPTAIN MARTIN WHITE, 1826, AND PUBLISHED AS ADMIRALTY CHART NO. 27 IN 1829 | The town and harbour of Dartmouth are about a mile up the fjord-like River Dart. The harbour has developed since the earliest times as a deep-water shelter traditionally for both fishing vessels and warships and has been a home to the navy since Edward III: the Britannia Royal Naval College has trained Royal Navy officers there since 1905.

This chart of Dartmouth Harbour, surveyed by Captain White, was engraved on copper by the Walker brothers, John and Charles, who ran their own firm in Castle Street, Holborn, London. (UKHO © British Crown Copyright)

His work was continued by his surveying assistant Lieutenant (later Commander) Henry Otter, who worked his way steadily westwards over the next 11 years, initially in the ketch *Sparrow* and then in the paddle steamer Avon. The advantage of paddle steamers was that they were able to maintain a steady position, relative to the sea bed and to the landmark used for a fix, in strong currents and tide-ways by judicious use of ahead and astern on the port and starboard paddles.

George Thomas was never commissioned, although he petitioned for and deserved it. He had cut his surveying teeth on the Schelde for a navy blockade back in 1809, and from 1811 spent 35 years surveying the Thames under Hurd. Then, appointed by Beaufort, he surveyed the North Sea, east coasts of England and Scotland with the Firth of Forth, and the Orkneys and Shetlands. He died still a Master 'in harness' on his way from the Orkneys to Woolwich for a spot of leave.

The task of surveying the River Thames was given to Commander Frederick Bullock. Starting at London Bridge he spent 17 years, completing his great survey in 1853 of the Thames Estuary to the Kentish Knock Sand, 30 miles to the east of the Nore, tying it in to the Ordnance Survey triangulation. He pioneered the main channels across the estuary, improving on Mackenzie's and Spence's earlier achievements, including the Prince's Channel, which was then carefully marked by three light vessels, the *Girdler*, Tongue and *Prince*'s, and a channel further to seaward which he named, not undeservedly, the Bullock Channel. Re-named today as the Duke of Edinburgh Channel it is the principal channel to the Port of London from the south.

The south coast was surveyed by Captain William Sheringham, who had started as an assistant to Beaufort in office, then assisting Slater in Scotland, before being given his own stretch to survey along the Welsh coast, then Cornwall in 1840. Promoted to Commander and given a paddle steamer, he made an urgent survey of Portsmouth and the Isle of Wight, until by 1853 he had joined up to Commander Martin White's earlier 1828 survey at Start Point in Devon to Falmouth, which he charted in the Shamrock. Commander George Williams, with experience

under Hewett in the *Fairy*, and with Frederick Beechey in the Irish Sea, surveyed the tricky seas around Land's End.

Ireland's east coast was covered by Commander William Mudge, and then by Robert Frazer, and the isolated west coast by Commander Richard Beechey, Frederick's younger brother, from 1835 to 1844, at which time Commander George Bedford, who had worked under George Thomas in Scotland, took over.

Captain Frederick Beechey used paddle steamers to survey the Irish Sea and became its acknowledged expert, advising on the rail and shipping routes between London and Dublin, designing improvements for Holyhead and Irish harbours, and on the postal service from Scotland to Ireland. He also surveyed the River Severn from Worcester to Minehead, which required special skill to cope with the rapid tidal streams.

Lieutenant Henry Denham took on another real problem. Liverpool by this time catered for 11,000 ships arriving and departing every year. The silting Mersey was diminishing the navigable height of water, limiting port operation to eight hours a day, and the situation was worsening. Denham intelligently surmised that the tide inducted a great quantity of water 3 miles wide. The traditional channels – the Formby and Rock Channels – were silting up, so there had to be another through which this well of water ebbed. Denham set about finding it, and by the end of the summer he had found and sounded the 'New Channel', unexpectedly in the middle of the estuary: a grateful Liverpool gave him the Freedom of the City and he was appointed their Marine Surveyor, the first to a British port. Today all British ports have their own marine surveyor, which has relieved the Hydrographic Office of this responsibility.

The chart abbreviations that Beaufort oversaw were standardised in 1835 and issued as a sheet to be dispensed with the charts. They endured until 1967 when fathoms were replaced by metres and the four-colour chart was adopted internationally. All depths were related to a 'sea-water table' level or chart datum that, at Low Water Spring Tides, would give the least amount of water over the sea bottom or rocks that a mariner would encounter. The design of the compass rose was standardised to show true north with the magnetic north taking the traditional fleur-de-lys arrowhead and the magnetic variation for that area shown. The abbreviations for the nature of the sea bed were also standardised; this is important for the mariner as the holding strength of the sea bed varies enormously. Other conventions included stippling to show drying mud and sand banks, underlined figures to show their height above low water and fathom-line symbols.

Beaufort's team, under his vision, leadership and encouragement, laid down the first composite, enduring survey of the British Isles and it remains the valid bedrock of all surveys thereafter.

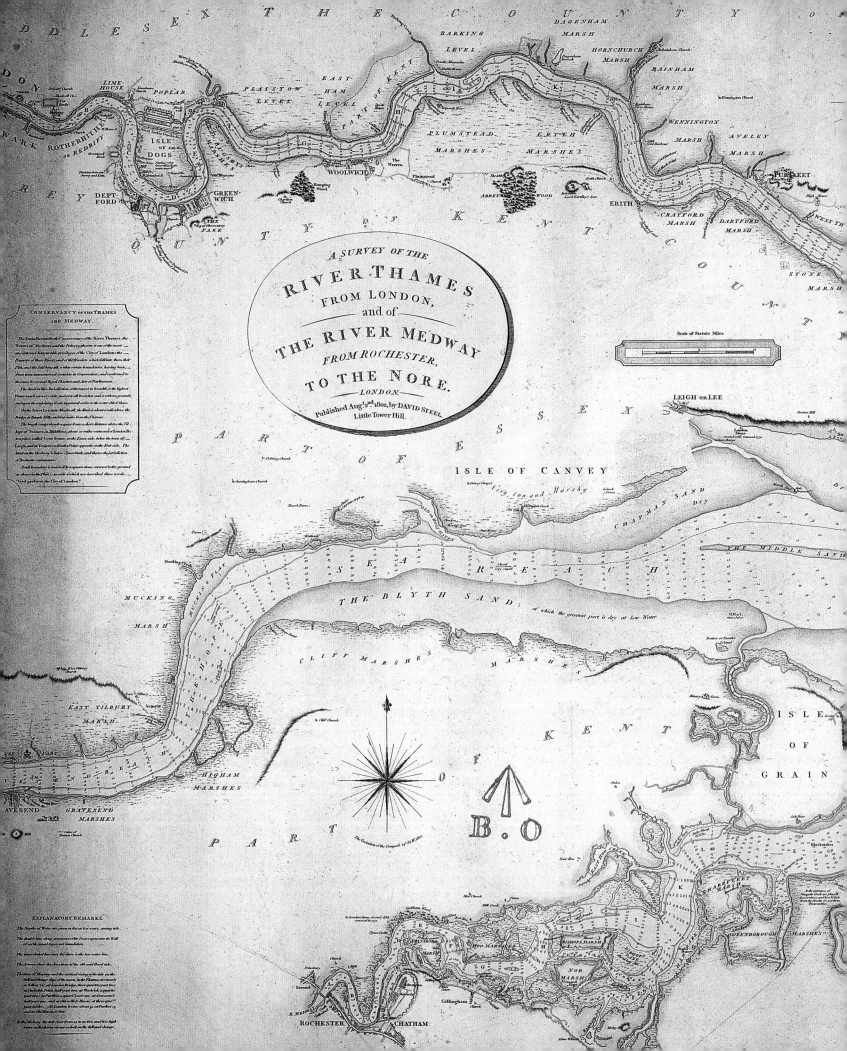

A SURVEY OF THE

RIVER THAMES

FROM LONDON,

and of

THE RIVER MEDWAY

FROM ROCHESTER,

TO THE NORE.

LONDON.

Published Aug.t 2.nd 1802, by DAVID STEEL,
Little Tower Hill.

CHAPTER II

LONDON
& THE THAMES ESTUARY

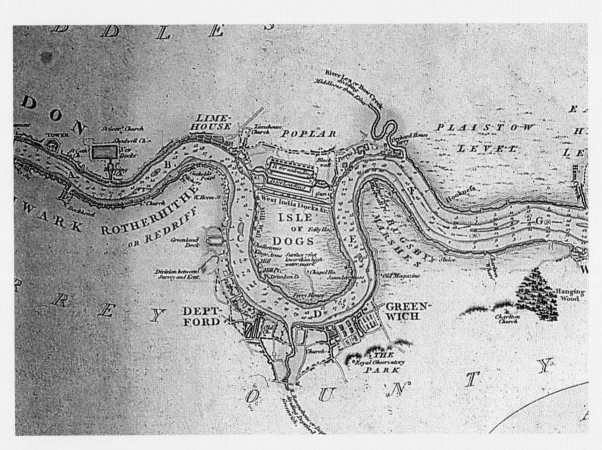

| LEFT & ABOVE DETAIL | A SURVEY OF THE RIVER THAMES AND THE RIVER
MEDWAY BY DAVID STEEL, 1802 | David Steel was a nautical publisher whose business succeeded
on the back of the publication of the List for the Royal Navy, from 1780 to 1816 – initially monthly, and
then quarterly – and other technical nautical works. He began publishing charts in 1782, working near
St Katherine's Dock, where he also taught navigation and sold navigational instruments, nautical books and
stationery. Part of his business acumen was in protecting his 'intellectual property rights', because he sued for
damages, as became prevalent at the time, against copyright for £3000 regarding a chart of 'the east coast of
England'. (The National Archives {PRO}: MPH1/578)

London straddles the River Thames 50 miles upriver from its mouth at the Nore, where the English Channel meets the North Sea. The key to London's evolution into one of the largest capital cities in the world lies, as with so many cities, in its river, named by Caesar as Tamesis. It rises in four headstreams – the Isis (or Windrush), the Churn, the Coln, and the Leach – on the south-eastern slopes of the Cotswold Hills in Gloucestershire, near Cheltenham. The streams converge on Oxford and flow generally south-east to Reading, through a gap in the Chiltern escarpment. The Thames, about 210 miles long, follows a generally eastern course through London. At London Bridge it has widened to about 870 feet and a few miles below Gravesend it expands into a wide estuary, between Whitstable and Foulness Point, some 18 miles across, and then enters the North Sea.

The other important river flowing into the Thames Estuary is the Medway, which rises in headstreams from northern East Sussex and south-eastern Surrey, and flows north-east past Tonbridge, turning north at Maidstone, and passing Rochester, to join the estuary opposite Southend-on-Sea giving natural opportunities for the naval dockyards at Chatham at the neck of the Medway estuary, and Sheerness at the mouth. Up to 5 miles wide, and very unevenly indented with many shoals and islands, the river's total length is 70 miles, and is navigable as far as Maidstone.

As the Thames by London is deep and still within the tidal zone it was an ideal place for berthing ships. The area was well-drained and low-lying with a geology suitable for brickmaking. There was soon a flourishing city called Londinium, the name of Celtic not Latin origin, in the area where the Monument now stands.

London began to flourish after the Roman conquest of Britain in AD 43, and it has remained the financial centre of Britain since then. Not surprisingly, little is known of London in the period widely called the Dark Ages, but Alfred the Great constructed a 'South-Werk' across the river to protect the ferry crossing.

With the Roman walls repaired and the ditch re-cut, Ealdorman Aethelred of Mercia established Aethelred's Hythe (Queenhythe) and Billingsgate Market and a new street system began to emerge.

William the Conqueror's successor, William Rufus, built the great hall at Westminster, reinforced the Tower of London and rebuilt the Thames bridge, which had been seriously damaged by flooding. In 1087, the city was devastated by a great fire and St Paul's was burnt to the ground (though soon rebuilt).

By the thirteenth century the crowded city was clustered along the riverbank, with a small settlement across the river in Southwark. Over the next three centuries trade prospered, the population outstripped any rival in England, and London became a major centre for importing and distributing goods to other parts of the country, and in Tudor times Henry VIII built his favourite residence at Greenwich.

In 1603 The East India Company was granted its Royal Charter. Its establishment was to dramatically change the profile of London. By 1621 the Company had docks at Deptford, and Blackwall at the north-east corner of the Isle of Dogs, where East Indiamen were built, provisioned and their cargo warehoused. Some idea of the scale of shipping can be garnered from the 4600 voyages made from London between 1600 and 1833 on behalf of the East India Company. The volume of just one product, tea, required 5 acres of warehousing with 4000 warehousemen and 400 clerks.

Charles I built the Queen's House at Greenwich and the Banqueting House at Whitehall, but the most significant civic achievement of his father James I's reign was the provision of a clean water supply for the capital under the New River Scheme.

The Great Fire of London of 1666 was devastating and changed the character of London forever. The new city gradually grew up with wider streets and, enforced by an Act of Parliament, brick and stone houses. A remarkable change had taken place between the chaos of the Civil War of 1642–51 and the stability of the Hanoverians. Thriving trade through the East India Company with the East and the colonies of North America needed docks to load and unload cargoes such as tea and silks and dockyards to repair the ships. By the time of Daniel Defoe's remarkable two-year *Tour Through the Whole Island of Great Britain* published in 1724 he was able to describe,

> ...that part of the River Thames, which is properly the harbour...is called the Pool, and it begins at the turning of the river out of Lime-House Reach, and extends to the Custom-House Keys. In this compass I have had the curiosity to count the ships as well as I could, en passant, and have found above two thousand sail of all sorts, not reckoning barges, lighters or pleasure-boats, and yatchs [sic]...

He includes ships lying at Deptford and Blackwall reaches and reports three wet docks for laying up, 22 dry docks for repairing and 33 yards for building merchant ships. Until 1750, London Bridge between the City and Southwark was the only bridge, but it was joined at that time by Westminster Bridge and nearly 20 years later by Blackfriars Bridge.

Industry, previously based in homes or small workshops, now required massive machinery and factories and moved to the suburbs and beyond. The Victorian construction of large-scale public railways, linking London to most of the major cities, transformed London's social and business life. The underground network and tramways followed. The growth of shipping and, in

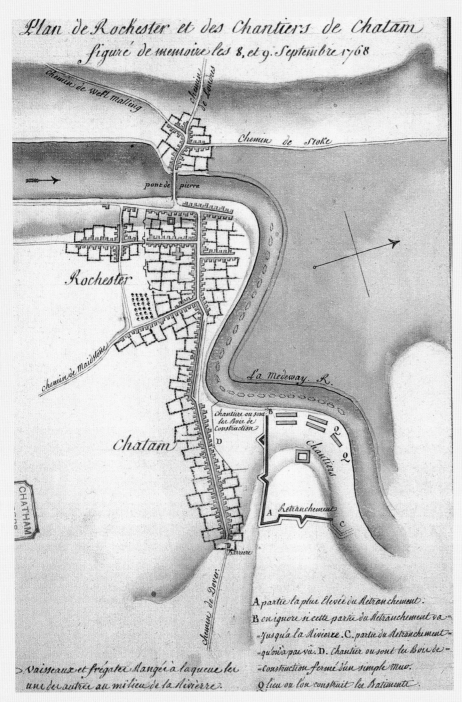

Plan de Rochester et des Chantiers de Chatam figuré de memoire les 8, et 9 Septembre 1768

A partie la plus elevée du Retranchement.

B on ignore si cette partie du Retranchement va jusqu'à la Rivierre. C. partie du Retranchement qu'on a pas vû. D. Chantier ou sont le Bois de Construction fermé d'un simple Mur. Q lieu ou l'on construit le Batiments.

Vaisseaux et frégates Mangés à la queue les unes des autres au milieu de la Rivierre.

| FRENCH MAP OF ROCHESTER AND CHATHAM, 1768 | This is one of a set of 25 charts drawn up from the notes of French spies seeking potential invasion ports and harbours. (The National Archives {PRO}: MR1/1111)

Today the area known as Docklands comprises almost 50 miles of quays. On the north bank of the Thames lie the districts of Wapping and Poplar, the Isle of Dogs, and the Royal Docks; on the south bank are the Surrey Docks. The area designated as the Port of London extends from Teddington Lock, which is about 10 miles west of the city, and the limit of tidal water, down river 93 miles to the Tongue light vessel. Ocean-going vessels, mainly cruise ships, can navigate to the upper part of the river through Tower Bridge.

During the nineteenth century the docks, at the hub of Britain's worldwide trade, made London the world's busiest port. Rapid decline set in after 1945, however, and the bulk container trade is now handled in Harwich and Rotterdam. On average 52 million tonnes of cargo are handled in the port of London annually, still making it Britain's largest general cargo. The whole region has been designated as a development area by the government under the title of 'Thames Gateway Initiative'.

Between Hampton Court and the Tower of London the river is now crossed by 20 road and nine rail bridges. The world's first bored tunnel was built under the Thames by Marc and Isambard Kingdom Brunel in 1825–42, while the latest bridge is the QEII Bridge opened by Elizabeth II in 1991, to take the north–south link of the M25 London orbital motorway.

The Thames has been the main source of drinking water for Greater London but the river has also been used as the city's sewage and industrial waste outlet. Joseph Bazalgette built the main sewage system between 1859 and 1875, diverting all domestic sewage and rainwater to outfalls further down river. Tides delayed the dispersal of the waste, however, and industrial pollution direct into the river continued until by 1949 the Thames in London had become completely devoid of oxygen. Stringent standards on the purity of all effluents since 1964 have raised the quality of Thames water.

By 1974, when the Port of London Authority handed over pollution control to the new Thames Water Authority, 82 species of freshwater and sea fish were to be found in waters previously inhabited only by the occasional eel, although storm drain effluent is still a threat to river life.

In 1984, responding then to tidal surges, rather than predicted global warming, the Thames Barrier was opened by Elizabeth II and consists of six steel gates each weighing up to 1500 tonnes, which are rotated 90 degrees into position from beneath the water.

particular, the construction of the famous clippers brought tea and other Far East exotica more rapidly from China to the Thames. The transport links were crucial in extending colonial domination and international trade and London had become very much the centre of the world's largest empire, as giant liners traversed the oceans with administrators, businessmen and troops.

| PANORAMIC VIEW OF LONDON ASCRIBED TO RALPH AGAS, C. 1560 | One of only three known examples of this map (shown here in two parts), this original woodcut is thought to have been made by Ralph Agas in the early 1560s, after the burning of the spire of St Paul's Cathedral in 1561. This is a copy of a later edition, presumed to have been made in 1633 from evidence in the cartouche at the lower right.

A glimpse of London in medieval times, the map follows the Thames from Westminster Hall around the almost 90-degree bend that the river makes at Charing Cross and east to Smithfield and the Tower of London, enclosing an area that stretches from just south of the river to the northern hills. It includes streets (some named), fields, waterways, quays, ships and boats, tenter grounds, human figures and animals. Various buildings are drawn with a bird's-eye view: St Paul's Cathedral, churches, gates, crosses, London Bridge, bull and bear baiting rings and windmills. The Arms of James I are at top left, with the arms of the City of London at top right, supported by two putti. The ornate cartouche at lower left gives a history of the city and the plain cartouche at lower right contains 10 lines of verse. Oriented with North to the top of the page, it has no scale, but is inscribed 'MDLX'. (The National Archives {PRO}: MPE1/25)

| RIGHT | This detail from the area around London Bridge shows, for example, 'Bylynges Gate' (Billingsgate) and various quays in the Pool of London.

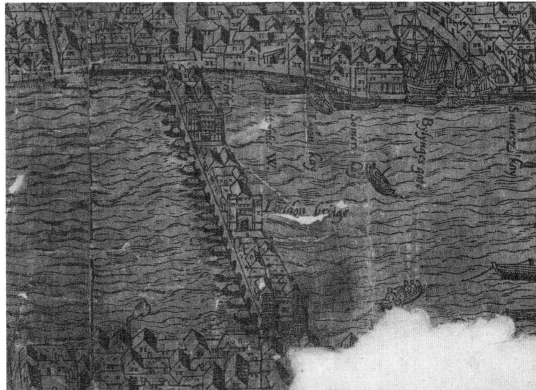

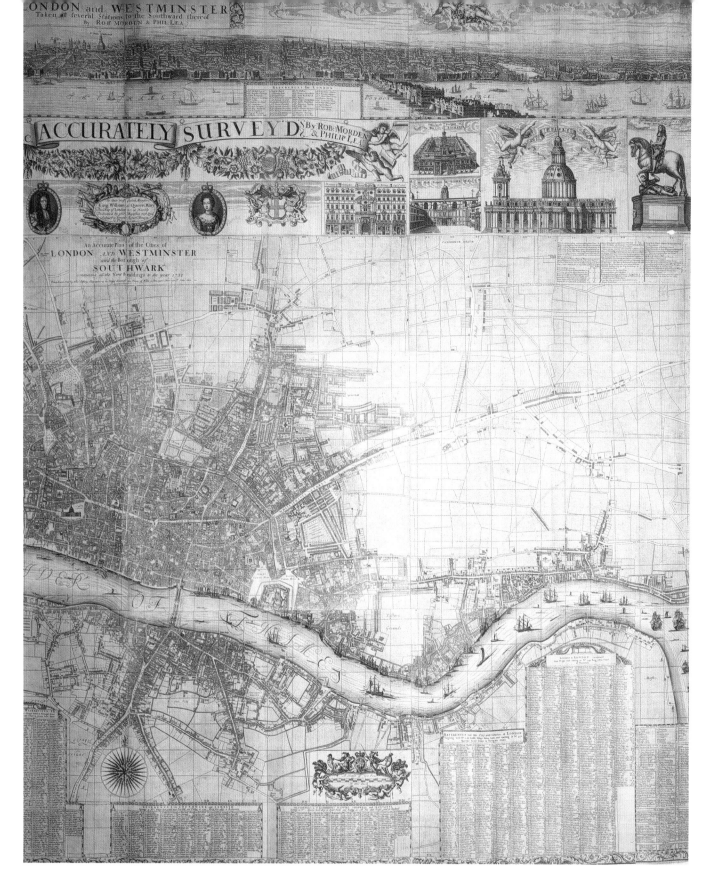

| LONDON, WESTMINSTER AND SOUTHWARK BY ROBERT MORDEN AND PHILIP LEA, C. 1700 | This intimate view of London and the River Thames gives a taste of the host of sailing vessels making for St Katherine's Stairs and to the jetties by the Customs House, near the Tower but below the only bridge – London Bridge. It shows a rebuilt Thames-side London after the Great Fire of 1666. Robert Morden and Philip Lea were independent cartographers with premises in Cheapside whose businesses flourished towards the end of the seventeenth century. They collaborated on this map of London, which dates to around 1700, although this version was printed later in 1732 by Thomas Jeffries, the outstanding cartographer and publisher of maps and charts appointed as Geographer to George III. (The National Archives {PRO}: MR1/694)

| RIGHT | WEST INDIA DOCKS, C. 1795 | This map shows the plans, with a scale of 1 inch to 4 chains, to build the West India Docks in the loop of the Thames called the Isle of Dogs from Limehouse Hole to Blackwall. The chart shows the dock at Deptford (lower left), gives depths of the river at various stages along its length and how the basins would be able accommodate 910 ships, with facilities for careening (pulling the vessel on to her side so as to clean the bottom). This was before the days of copper-bottoming when the Navy Board's policy was to careen ships of the line three to four times a year, while cruisers and frigates were meant to be docked every six weeks. (The National Archives {PRO}: MR1/237)

| BELOW | PLAN OF LONDON DOCKS, WAPPING, 1831 | This plan of the London Docks at Wapping, with a scale of 1 inch to about 440 feet, shows St Katherine's and Tobacco Docks, the Tobacco and Sugar Warehouses, and depths, clearly by a land surveyor, marked in feet. It is interesting to see the reference to the safe chart datum set by Trinity House noted with depths 1 foot 6 inches below an 'ordinary Spring [low] Tide'. The engineer is noted as Henry R Palmer. The plan was drawn by I B Surgey and engraved by E Turrell. (The National Archives {PRO} MPD1/65)

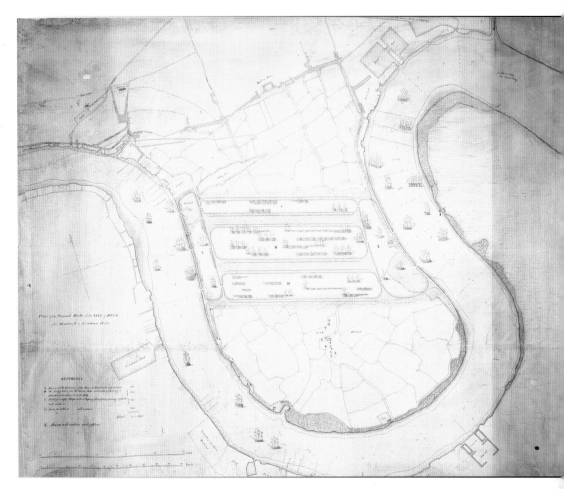

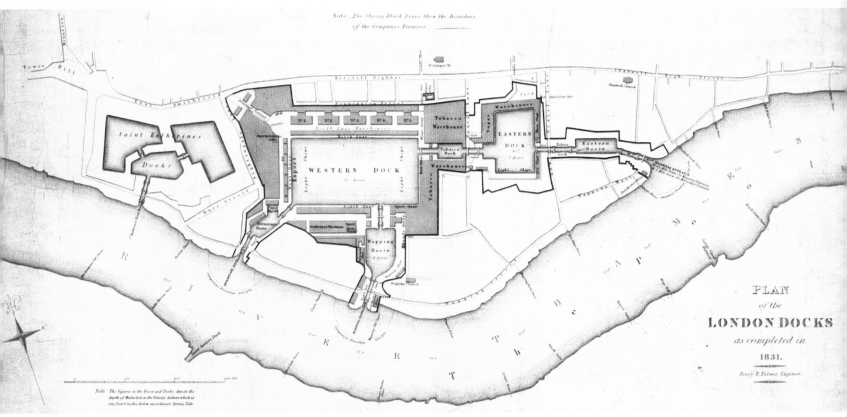

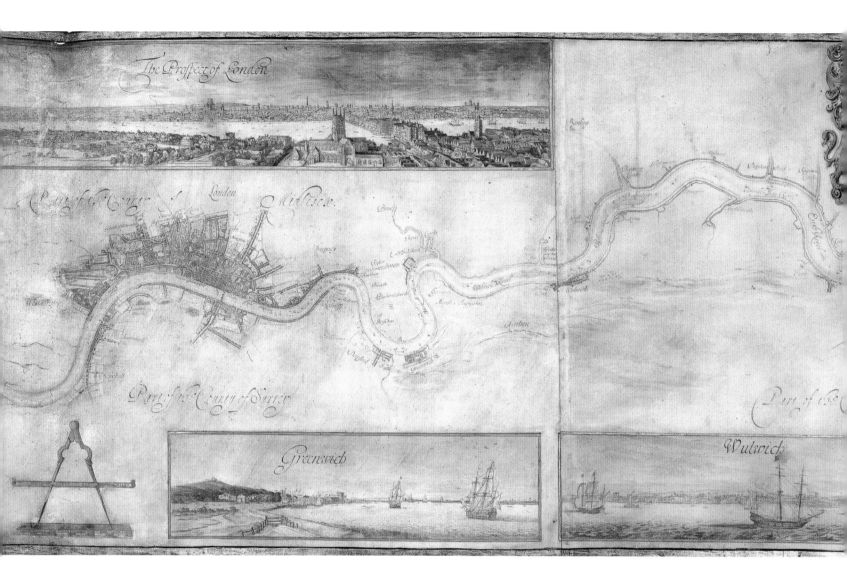

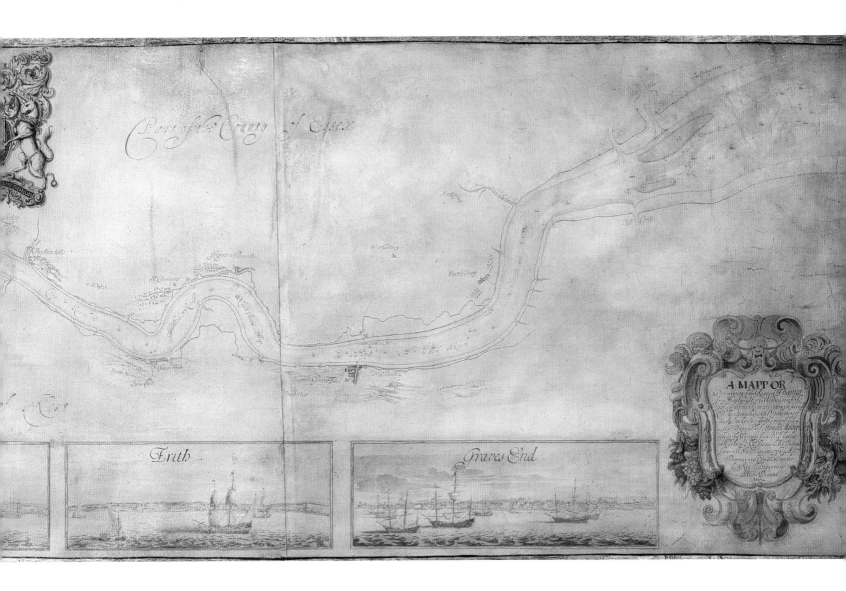

| **THE RIVER THAMES FROM WESTMINSTER TO TILBURY WITH VIEWS OF LONDON, GREENWICH, WOOLWICH, ERITH AND GRAVESEND, 1662** | The 'Prospect of London' view looks north across the River Thames, showing London Bridge crossing from Southwark to the city, with St Paul's to the right and Westminster Abbey to the left. The view of Greenwich, so linked with British naval history, shows the Queen's House, now part of the National Maritime Museum. The Royal Observatory was not built until 1675. Woolwich, along with Deptford, was a naval yard founded in the sixteenth century, well placed for London and protected from attack. But they became outdated as larger ships of the line drew too much water to be able to sail there for refits unless they unloaded all their guns and stores at Gravesend, which remained an ordnance depot until the early nineteenth century. Gravesend was described by Charles Dickens (Jnr) in his *Dictionary of the Thames* in 1887 as the gateway to London, and it complemented Tilbury Fort opposite on the north bank of the Thames. Erith now has a deep-water jetty for large container ships to unoad, but had been built up on the mud flats of north Kent near Bexley as a port so that in the seventeenth century and up to about 1800, when the Thames would silt up, ships loaded and unloaded and the navy fleet lay up there. It was used as a royal 'staging post', too: for example, Charles II saw his daughter leave there in 1667 for her marriage to William of Orange (later William III). (The National Archives {PRO}: WORK38/331)

| ISLE OF SHEPPEY, C. 1572 |

This map of the Isle of Sheppey shows houses and churches, trees, water channels, marshes and hills, windmills and beacons, including Queensborough Castle and town and the town of Minster, long before Samuel Pepys ordered a Royal Dockyard to be built on the Isle. The River Medway, Isle of Grain and north Kent coast are sketched in, and Swaleness Fort is marked. Around the coast there are seven ships and a man in a boat, drawn to indicate the ferry to the mainland. Reference notes in the fretwork cartouche indicate anchorages and passages for ships.

Although Latin was no longer the official language of the English church by the sixteenth century, it was the established language for scholars and the law. So it was to be expected that this map, extracted from a volume containing two surveys of Lord Cheney's possessions on Sheppey, and undertaken to support the sequestration of his property on the grounds of its importance for the defence of the Isle of Sheppey, should be annotated in Latin. As such, note the scale bar, surmounted by dividers, with its legend in Latin, which gives 3 inches to 1 mile, and the four winds *Aquilo* (North), *Auster* (South), *Oriens* (East) and *Occidens* (West), which are named in lieu of a compass rose. (The National Archives {PRO}: MPF1/240)

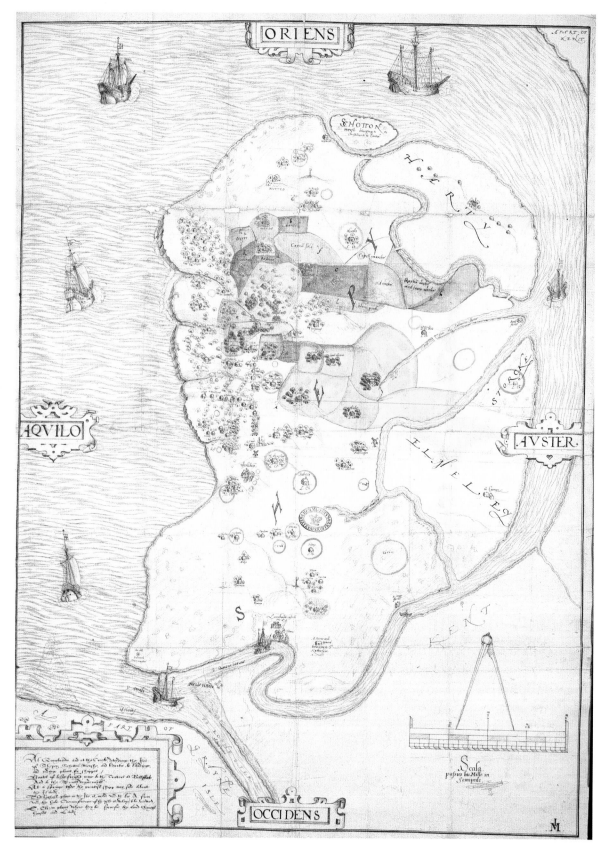

| RIGHT | PROPOSED WORKS TO STRENGTHEN THE SECURITY OF
THE DOCKYARD AT SHEERNESS, 1825 | This plan of the intended
strengthening of one of Britain's most important dockyards also shows much of
the existing docks and basins, with the town and owners' names and buildings.

Samuel Pepys, as First Secretary to the Admiralty, ordered the Royal Dockyard to
be built at the entrance to the Thames, partly in response to the Dutch threat. It would
probably have been more important if it had not flooded during construction, but was
favoured over the upriver yards, which were difficult to get to and so tended to be used for
building ships and main refits.

Today Sheerness is an important commercial port and the main town of the Isle of
Sheppey, owing much to its origins as a Royal Naval Dockyard town. (The National
Archives {PRO}: MR1/1339)

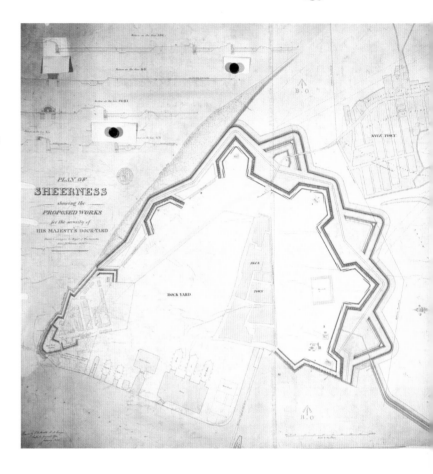

| BELOW | CHART OF THE RIVER MEDWAY FROM ROCHESTER TO
SHEERNESS, 1688 | This chart, signed by Captain Greenvile Collins, was probably
made at the request of Trinity House as part of his epic seven-year *Great Britain's Coasting
Pilot*. With Collins' characteristic thoroughness, using, as required in his instructions, a
chain and bearings of headlands to create the survey, it shows intriguing details, such as
the chain or 'boome' across the river at Upnor Castle, built in 1559 to protect Chatham
Dockyard, which the Dutch under Admiral de Ruyter broke through, sailing on to
Rochester Bridge (also shown) and capturing and firing the English fleet on 11 June
1667 during the Second Anglo-Dutch War; the salt pans on the Isle of Grain, the
soundings and the nature of the sea bed and anchorages. Batteries and ships at the
mouth of the Medway give a sense of scale. One of Collins' innovations was to mark
out the low water line. Approximate scale is noted as 3.17 inches to 1 mile. The
attractive compass rose shows the chart orientation with South towards the top of
the page. (The National Archives {PRO}: MPHH1/25)

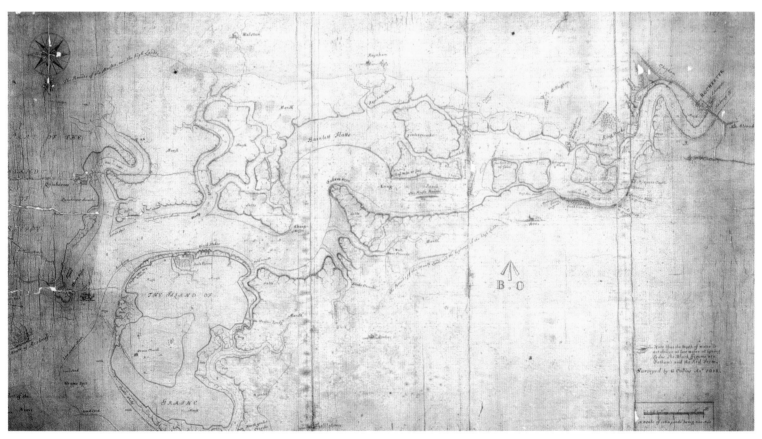

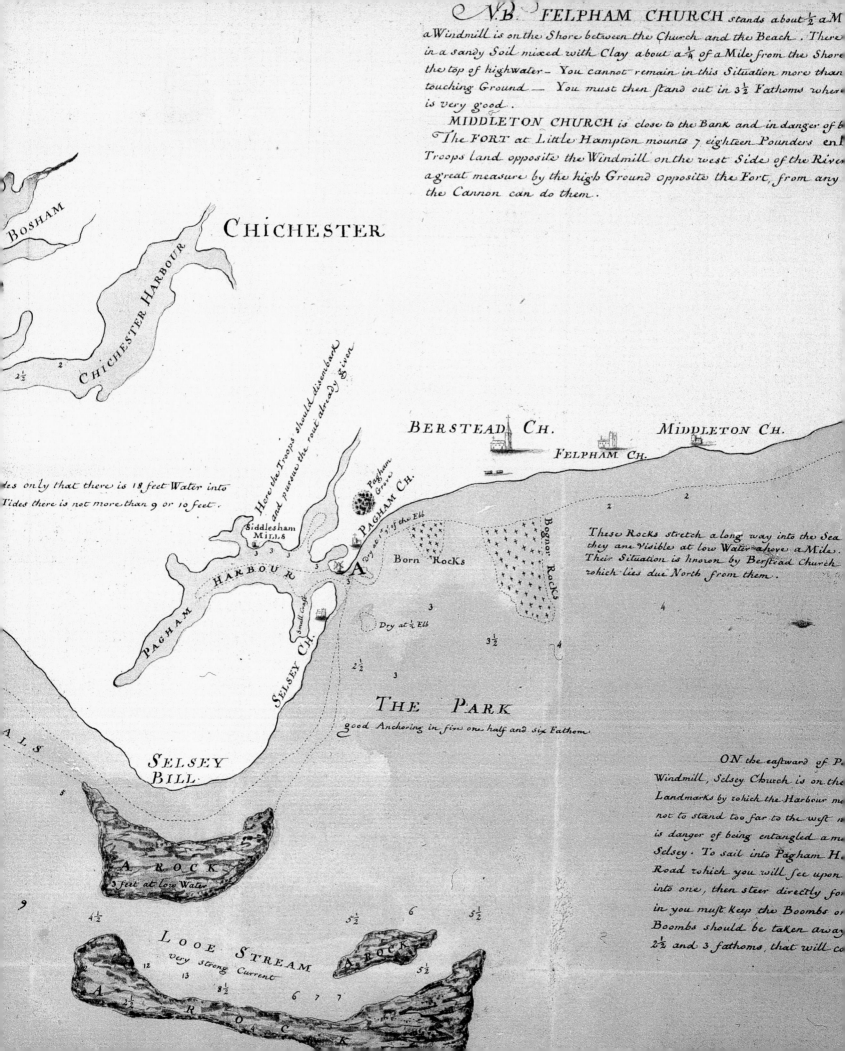

CHAPTER III

THE SOUTH COAST OF ENGLAND

Shore,
choring
ms about
thout
oring

l away.
If
be Covered in
Shot from

ARUNDELL RIVER
by the River 6 Miles to
Arundell by the Road 4

LITTLE
HAMPTON

......Into Arundell River 11 F.
Water at Spring Tides; at
Water there is not more
than 2 feet.

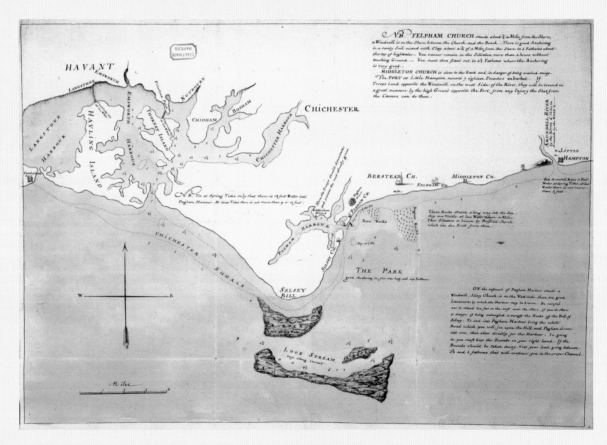

| LEFT DETAIL & ABOVE | MANUSCRIPT CHART OF HAVANT, CHICHESTER, SELSEY BILL AND ARUNDEL, 1768 | This chart of Selsey Bill and the surrounding coast from Langstone Harbour to Littlehampton comes from William Pitt the Elder's papers of the time. Alongside detailed information for ships such as depths and navigational approach advice, it states where troops could land in Pagham Harbour.

Selsey Bill, like Portland Bill, was once an island with a Roman port and a Saxon cathedral. The cathedral was destroyed by the sea, and the bishopric moved to Chichester in 1075. By the fourteenth century Chichester was one of the 10 leading English ports, until ship size precluded its use in the seventeenth century, and Emsworth came into its own. (The National Archives {PRO}: MR1/1111{24})

our stands a
these are good
Be careful
, if you do there
ocks off the Bill of
g the rohite
nd Pagham Grove
our. In going
t hand. If the
r lead going between
in the proper Channel.

Think of coming home by sea to England and, as Dame Vera Lynn sang for the men fighting in the Second World War, you think of 'the white cliffs of Dover'. These iconic chalk limestone cliffs that run from Kent to the Isle of Wight were the first bastion against invaders of these shores from the Romans, the Normans, the Spanish and the French, to the German forces of the twentieth century.

For those 'who go down to the sea in ships and make their business on great waters' the south coast offers a multiple choice of harbours and today many activities centre on them. Cross-channel and other ferries head to France from many ports along the south coast, such as Dover, Newhaven, Southampton, Lymington, Poole and Weymouth. Other harbours are home to yacht and pleasure boats and many have their own yacht and cruising clubs. Some of these are famous and elite, such as the Royal Yacht Squadron at Cowes on the Isle of Wight or the Royal Southern Yacht Club based at the entrance of the Hamble River from Southampton Water, and most brook a wider membership with smaller dinghies and power boats.

To take our 'tour' logically starting from the eastern end of the Thames Estuary, which can be thought of as marked by the crumbling cliffs of Reculver, we start at Margate, which had been popular in Georgian times with Londoners coming by boat, but boomed with access via the Victorian railway that brought families to the seaside. Turning south, Ramsgate was one of the feeder towns for ships anchored at the Downs as they waited, sometimes for weeks, for a favourable wind to head west along the Channel; Sandwich was the favoured royal port to sail to France until the retreating sea cut it off in the sixteenth century; but Deal was the nearer harbour to the Downs and provided help, at a price, when storms dragged ship's anchors. The 'hovellers' brought large sheet anchors precariously balanced in their small boats, and rowed or sailed to an endangered ship to bend a safety anchor on to their cable. An altruistic example was the Great Storm of 1703 when 360 ships were lost and 1500 seamen drowned, but the Deal longshoremen saved some 200 lives. This 'invasion coast' needed protection over the centuries and Henry III had three great castles built at Sandown – now lost to the sea – Deal and Walmer, where the Lord Warden of the Cinque Ports still has his official residence. Originally there were five cinque ports – Sandwich, Dover, Hythe, Romney, and Hastings – and later Rye and Winchelsea were added. The oldest charter dates from 1278 and until the sixteenth century the Cinque Ports were charged with furnishing ships and men for the service of the Crown in times of war, making a sort of medieval navy. In return, they were given privileges in tolls and profitable jurisdiction over the eastern waters of the Channel. Their importance declined with the growth of Plymouth and

| PLAN OF THE COAST FROM SHOREHAM TO PORTSMOUTH WITH SELSEY BILL BY LIEUTENANT HENRY P ANSON, 1765 |
From the mid eighteenth century sea-going officers were required to send in to the Admiralty surveys of where they had been, although they could sell copies to the commercial cartographers around the Minories in London. This was one such chart. It is crude in appearance, with no latitude or longitude, just a simple scale, and the buoys marking the shoals. (Admiralty Library Manuscript Collection: Vz 11/21)

Bristol when oceanic voyages proliferated and a formal navy was fashioned under Henry VII and Henry VIII.

Folkestone was a lesser medieval port, but was revived, as were so many, by the Victorian railway, and the 1970s enlargement as a passenger ferry terminal.

From a port so big its fishermen rivalled those of Great Yarmouth, and had four churches to accommodate their faith (medieval seamen had a strong religious belief, so dangerous was their profession), Hythe's demise was caused by the shifting shingle which choked her passage to the Channel. The 28-mile Royal Military Canal, cut along the inner edge of Romney Marsh in 1804–07 to a width of 60 feet and a depth of 9 feet, joined Hythe to Rye, but was for defensive use to move troops in the event of an invasion, rather than an attempt to re-invent Hythe as a port; but it was used for commercial traffic until 1909.

These historic ports compensate for the blander pebbled beaches of Eastbourne and Brighton. However, Eastbourne has the highest of the southern white chalk cliffs, with Beachy Head rising up majestically to 536 feet, although slowly giving ground to the sea at about 3 feet a year. And Brighton is where the British invented the seaside holiday in the seventeenth century, when fashionable society took to the waters (modestly in bathing machines) boosted by the Prince Regent's (later George IV) passion, the multi-domed Brighton Pavilion; his own pleasure palace. For the hoi polloi in Victorian times Brighton built two piers.

Further along the coast is George III's favourite resort, Bognor Regis, and it was also enjoyed by Queen Victoria, although she favoured Osborne House on the Isle of Wight, and George V liked it, too. Continuing on, we come to the small peninsula of Selsey Bill, once an island with a Roman fort, that pushes south into the English Channel and is topped with a lighthouse. The coast turns north again to the estuarine area, with flat-land birds nesting there, around the sailing Mecca of Hayling Island, Bosham and Emsworth, which took over the Selsey trade when it silted up.

Richard I ordered the construction of a dockyard at Portsmouth in 1194, but its greatest achievement came at the beginning of the twentieth century with the building of the Dreadnoughts. It lost the Royal Dockyard title in 1984, but the naval base has remained the home port of the Royal Navy. Portsmouth is also where the ferries leave for the island that lies across the Solent. The Isle of Wight was not always an island. Aeons ago, the low-lying ground around Portsmouth, Langstone and Chichester drained the chalk streams flowing southward and a chalk ridge that ran from the Isle of Purbeck to the Isle of Wight took the waters along its north side in a valley into which the sea broke, eroding the softer rock of the old Frome Valley, forming the Solent and isolating the Isle of Wight. A fleet could anchor at Spithead, sheltered from south-westerlies, awaiting any word that the French had slipped out of Brest. Today the Solent is one of the busiest waterways in the world with a mix of oil tankers to the refinery at Fawley, container ships and liners to the port at Southampton and innumerable yachts and pleasure boats. It is the scene for almost too much sailing, from the prestigious America's Cup, the Round the Island Race, to the many local yacht club races organised by the Royal Southampton, Southern, Lymington and Cowes Yacht Clubs to name a few.

From Studland Bay in Dorset to Exeter there are 95 miles of 185-million-year-old geology, known as the Jurassic coast, with many idiosyncratic marvels, such as the limestone arch at Durdle Door, carved out by wave action, and the almost circular, intimate beach at Lulworth Cove, formed by the sea eroding a gap in the limestone cliffs, past Portland Bill and Chesil Beach to the beach by Charmouth, where the first complete skeleton of an ichthysaurus, a prehistoric reptile 21 feet long, was discovered in 1811, and Lyme Regis where the ammonites fall away from the eroding cliffs on to the beach.

By Berry Head the coast embraces Torbay – the English Riviera. Brixham, where William III landed in 1688 to accept the Crown of England, nestles by Berry Head, supporting its harbour with the remains of a fishing fleet that in 1850 was boasted as England's biggest, with over 270 brigs, schooners, smacks and, of course. the Brixham trawler. It has been somewhat re-generated by the deep-water jetty, built in 1971.

Dartmouth is still the naval college for training Royal Navy cadet officers, but was originally a fishing harbour that is now a haven packed with yachts. Further west along the coast is Slapton Sands, actually shingle, which was built up by the sea into a bar that runs 5 miles north from Start Point. It was ideal as the rehearsal beach for D-Day in 1944, although tragically things went wrong when nine German torpedo boats from Cherbourg stumbled on a flotilla of eight LSTs exercising on the coast and sank three of them with heavy loss of life.

Between Plymouth, home to another naval dockyard and busy port, and Land's End there are many attractive small harbours and ports beloved of the tourist and visitor including Looe, Polperro, Fowey, Mevagissey, Falmouth, and Mount's Bay with Penzance, Britain's most westerly town, which used to be the centre for tin exports and pilchard catches, and the pretty harbours of Mousehole and Newlyn, Cornwall's principal fishing port dating from the fifteenth century. When the railway arrived, allowing fish to be delivered to London within seven hours, the jetties were lengthened to take the increasing numbers of fishing boats. Newlyn's appealing views across Mount's Bay and the tidal island of St Michael's Mount, an offshore granite boss, attracted artists from the 1880s onwards and the Newlyn School of Art was established.

Ships crossing the Atlantic from America, or bringing trade from Spain or the Mediterranean, would often see the Lizard Lighthouse, the southernmost point of the English mainland, built on the 200-foot high 'serpentine' rock cliffs. Smugglers used the havens on this coast, cocking a snook at the 'revenue men' with such village port names as Coverack meaning 'hideaway' in local dialect. Whilst most stories of the Cornish wreckers are probably exaggerations the locals were not overly thrilled when a beacon was put on the Lizard in 1619. The Vicar in Scilly, Reverend Troutbeck, led prayers with his own: 'Dear God, we pray not that wrecks should happen, but if it be Thy will that they do, we pray Thee let them be to the benefit of Thy poor people of Scilly'.

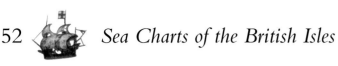

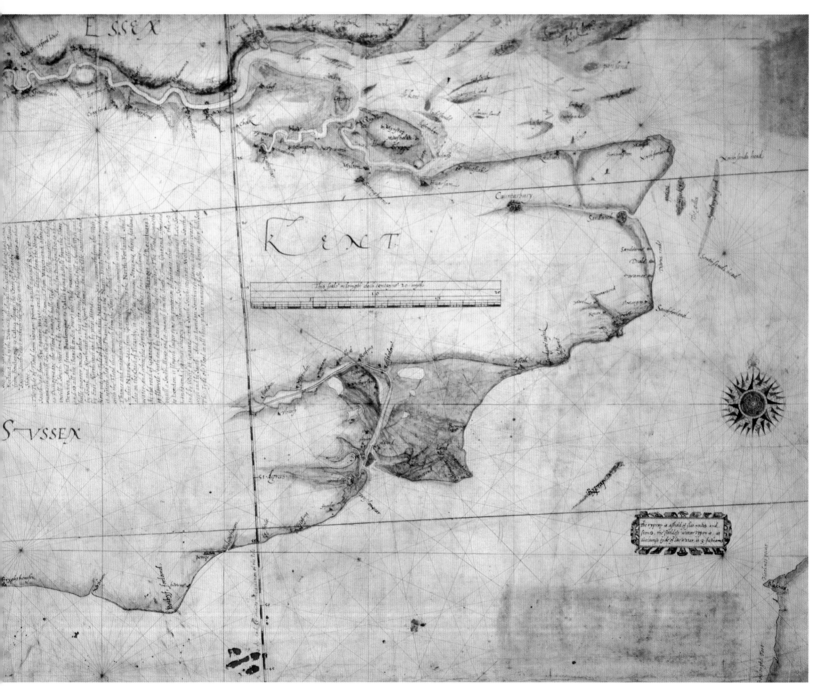

| KENT AND THE EAST SUSSEX COAST BY WILLIAM BOROUGH, C. 1580 | Borough was one of the band of seamen who loyally served Elizabeth I, culminating in his command of the Bonavolia against the Spanish Armada in 1588. He began his naval service as an ordinary seaman on board the Edward Bonaventure in 1553. By 1570, as a naval officer, he fought against pirates in the Gulf of Finland, and then took command of the Lion under Sir Francis Drake during the operation at Cadiz in 1587 known as 'singeing the King of Spain's beard', which was intended to pre-empt the Spanish Armada. However, he dared to question Drake's wisdom in attacking Lagos, which put him into the promotional backwater. Instead, he concentrated on navigation, writing *Instructions for the discovery of Cathy* and *A discourse on the Variation of the Compass* in about 1590.

Although not of the Thames School of 'platte-makers', Borough is acknowledged as one of the important Elizabethan chartmakers, and certainly had the experience to back up the practice. His brother, Stephen, was also a well-respected navigator and explorer. (By permission of the British Library: Cotton Augustus I.i.17)

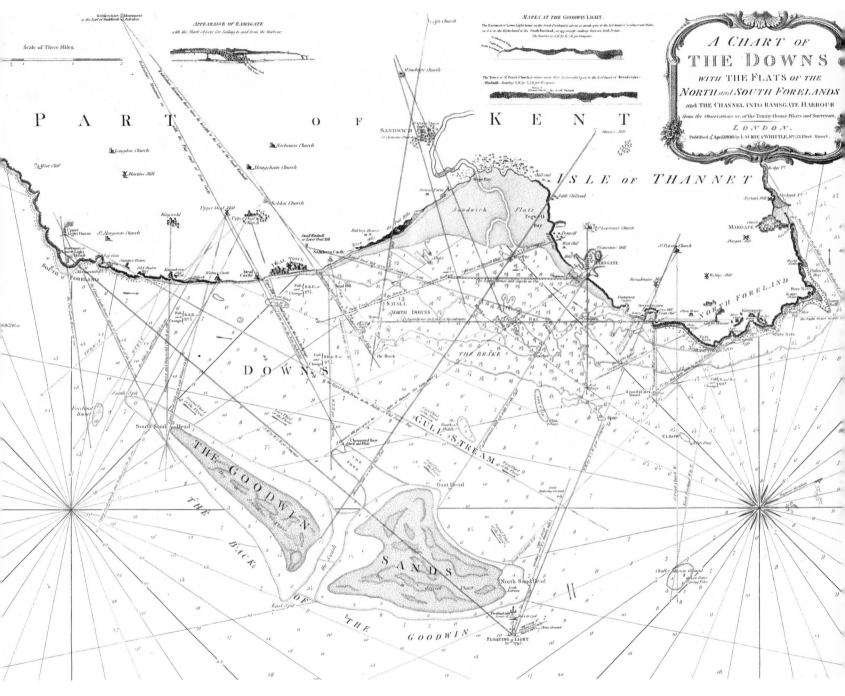

| THE DOWNS, PUBLISHED BY LAURIE AND WHITTLE IN 1800 |

The Downs provided a natural anchorage for sailing vessels: the land protected it from westerlies and the Goodwin Sands from easterlies. Merchant ships awaiting a favourable wind to sail into London or for an easterly wind to take them down the Channel could congregate there. There were no harbours nearby: Sandwich had silted up centuries before, Ramsgate was extended, completed in 1792 and could take up to 200 merchant ships, while warships were supplied from Deal, a beach port where boats landed on the steep pebbles. The navy used it as an anchorage from which to watch the North Sea and Dutch ports during the Napoleonic War. But it is a dangerous area as the sands continuously shift, and it was not properly marked until Trinity House buoyed it. Graeme Spence had charted it under Dalrymple's aegis, and Frederick Bullock's survey was more thorough, but each successive survey, of 1865 and 1887 by Captain William Archdeacon, and again by Captain George Pirie in HMS Triton in 1896, showed extensive changes to the Goodwin Sands, swinging eastwards for a century until 1865 then westwards towards the coast. (UKHO © British Crown Copyright)

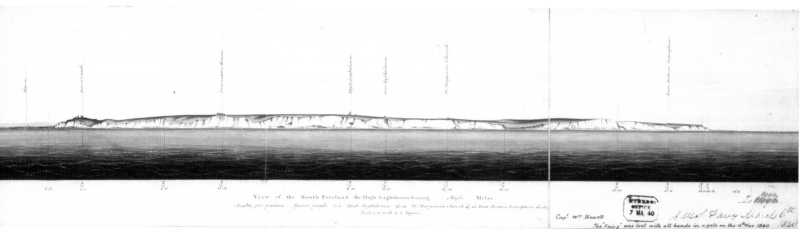

| **ABOVE** | **NAVIGATIONAL VIEW OF SOUTH FORELAND POINT AND THE KENT COAST, 1840** | This classic view of the English south coast includes Dover Castle, St Margaret's Church, some 'Preventative' (Customs) Houses and the semaphore station at East Boton.

Tragedy has always played a part in the history of surveying and the death of Captain William Hewett in the North Sea in the nineteenth century is an example of this. Notes regarding the loss of HMS Fairy with all hands off Lowestoft in 1840 are written on to the view. (UKHO © British Crown Copyright)

| OPPOSITE | SEA MAP OF RYE HARBOUR BY JOHN PROUEZ, C. 1572 | This sea map of Rye Harbour dates to about 1572 and was attached to a petition to the court of November 1595. Showing the country and marshland around Rye and Winchelsea, it includes the channels from the sea to the two towns packed with ships and boats, and with buildings drawn in perspective. Although it has no scale shown, the four compass roses show the chart's construction to be along the lines of a portolan chart, with a grid of rhumb lines drawn as the guide.

Today Rye, an attractive town with medieval houses, streets and walls, once lapped by the sea, is 2 miles inland. 'The sea giveth and the sea taketh away'. (The National Archives {PRO}: MPF1/212)

| ABOVE | FRENCH MAP OF DOVER, 1768 | This is one of the 25 maps prepared by French Intelligence with a view to an invasion of Britain. Drawn from memory, with a few gaps, it is nonetheless adequate for an invading fleet to use, showing the mole, fortifications, harbour, rocks and low water mark. (The National Archives {PRO}: MR 1/1111{3})

| RIGHT | VIEW OF HASTINGS BY W H BARTLETT, 1842 | Hastings developed in Saxon times and was the most westerly of the Cinque Ports. It lost its harbour to the build-up of sand and shingle, like many of the others, during the Middle Ages, and was reduced to a beach port. In Victorian times, colliers and trading vessels would be run up on the beach at high tide, swiftly unloaded, and floated off on the next high tide. (By permission of the British Library: 1502/320 Vol. I)

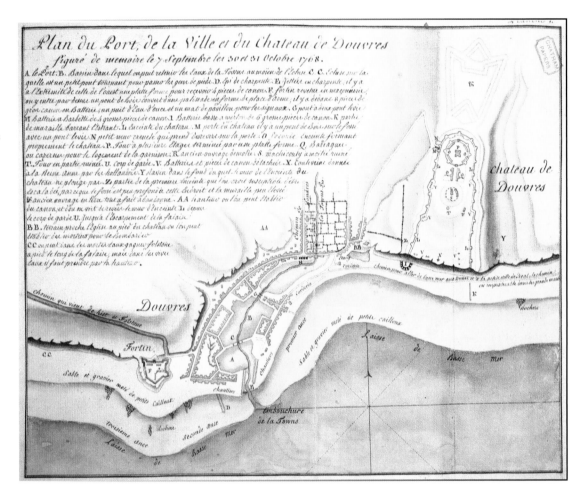

| **MARITIME MAP OF SUSSEX FROM CHICHESTER TO BRIGHTON,**
1778–80 | This is an unusual map as both the land and sea are equally represented.
The detail shows how small 'Brighthelmstone' (Brighton) was compared to say Chichester.
Soundings in fathoms are given and anchorages recommended. The cartouche around the
perimeter clearly should ensure personal interest as anyone who was anyone is mentioned.
The detail on land is impressively comprehensive and comparisons with today are
interesting. (The National Archives {PRO}: MR1/1169)

B R I T I S H

SCALE of Three Statute Miles

To
SIR CECIL BISHOP,
of Parham Place in the County Bart
This Second Plate of the County of SUSSEX
is respectfully dedicated by your most Obed.
and humble Servants
Tyrrell & W. Gardner

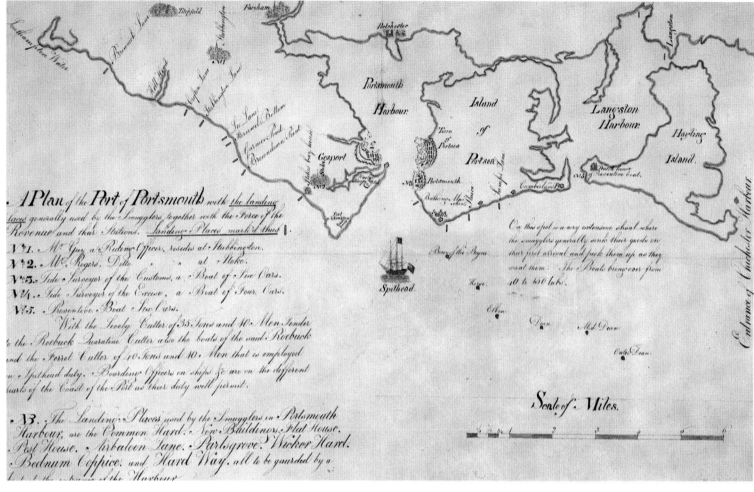

| ABOVE | PLAN OF PORTSMOUTH AND THE LANDING PLACES 'GENERALLY USED BY SMUGGLERS' BY RICHARD POPINJAY, 1587 | This plan, originally held with the Crown's state papers, includes parts of Hampshire around Portsmouth and shows Hayling Island to Titchfield and inland to Catherington at a scale of about 1 inch to 1 mile. Popinjay was Elizabeth I's Royal Surveyor. He also prepared a map of the defences of the Isle of Wight, Hampshire and Dorset against the expected Armada. It is a fascinating document produced for Customs that shows which landing places smugglers might use, details of where the smugglers would 'sink their goods on their first arrival and pick them up as they want them', with details of the revenue cutters and men, and some charming little drawings of the towns and churches. (The National Archives {PRO}: MPF1/134)

| RIGHT | View of Portsmouth from the Saluting Gun platform by W H Bartlett, 1842. (By permission of the British Library: 1502/320 Vol. I)

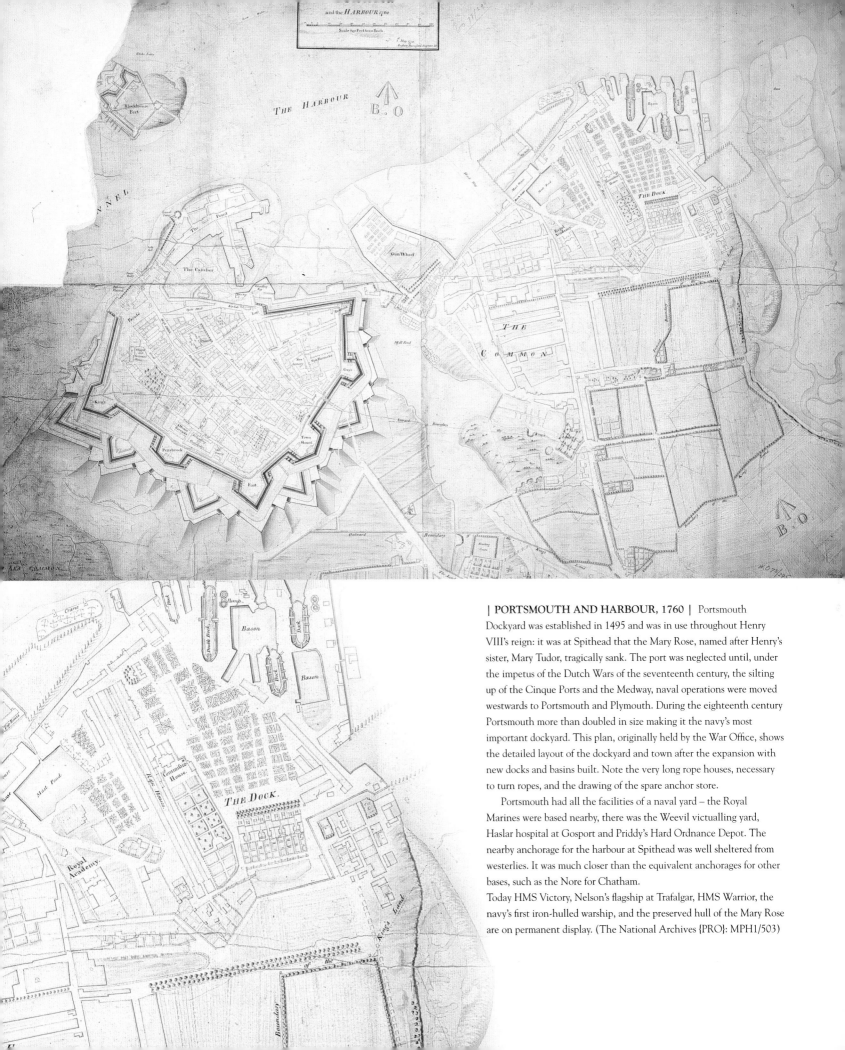

and the *HARBOUR* 1760.

Scale 340 Feet to an Inch.

1st May 1772.
Andrew Dury[?] Engineer[?]

THE HARBOUR

| PORTSMOUTH AND HARBOUR, 1760 | Portsmouth

Dockyard was established in 1495 and was in use throughout Henry
VIII's reign: it was at Spithead that the Mary Rose, named after Henry's
sister, Mary Tudor, tragically sank. The port was neglected until, under
the impetus of the Dutch Wars of the seventeenth century, the silting
up of the Cinque Ports and the Medway, naval operations were moved
westwards to Portsmouth and Plymouth. During the eighteenth century
Portsmouth more than doubled in size making it the navy's most
important dockyard. This plan, originally held by the War Office, shows
the detailed layout of the dockyard and town after the expansion with
new docks and basins built. Note the very long rope houses, necessary
to turn ropes, and the drawing of the spare anchor store.

Portsmouth had all the facilities of a naval yard – the Royal
Marines were based nearby, there was the Weevil victualling yard,
Haslar hospital at Gosport and Priddy's Hard Ordnance Depot. The
nearby anchorage for the harbour at Spithead was well sheltered from
westerlies. It was much closer than the equivalent anchorages for other
bases, such as the Nore for Chatham.

Today HMS Victory, Nelson's flagship at Trafalgar, HMS Warrior, the
navy's first iron-hulled warship, and the preserved hull of the Mary Rose
are on permanent display. (The National Archives {PRO}: MPH1/503)

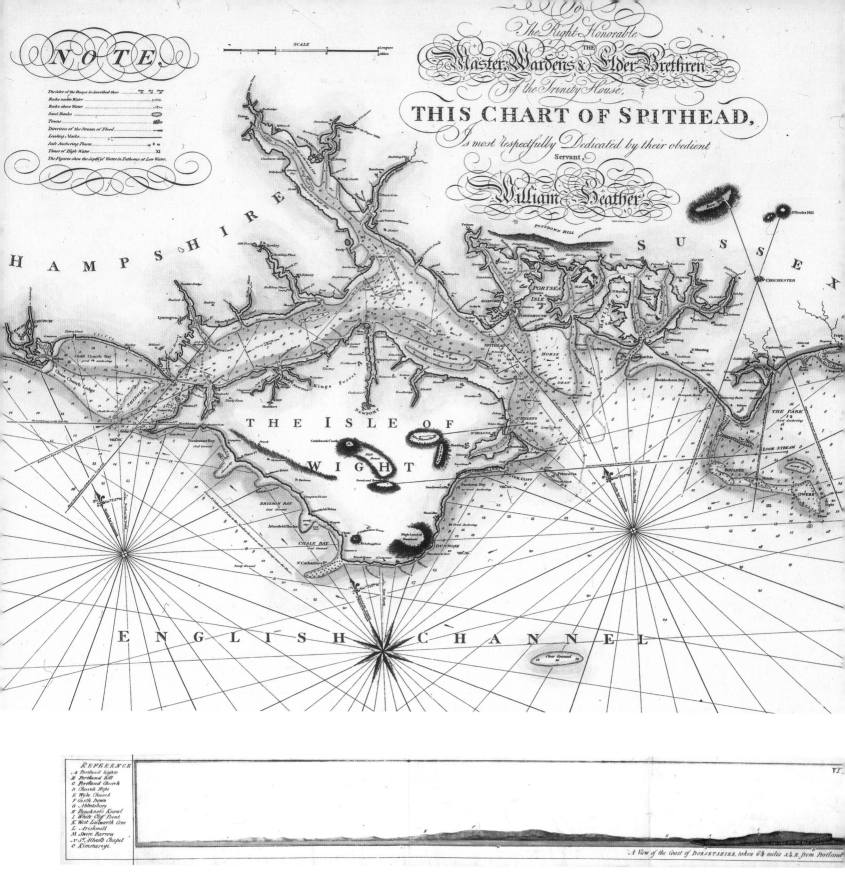

| ABOVE | NAVIGATIONAL VIEW OF THE DORSET COAST IN A PANORAMA FROM ST ALBAN'S HEAD (AND CHAPEL) TO LYME REGIS BY LIEUTENANT MURDOCH MACKENZIE, 1786 | Painted from Lyme Bay 6¼ miles south-east of Portland Bill by Mackenzie, who was appointed by the Admiralty to survey much of the southern coastal waters of England. He has keyed with letters the principal visual features of the coast: from Portland Bill in the centre, along Chesil Beach to Lyme Regis in the distance to the left, and to the right of the Bill, Lulworth Cove and eastwards to St Alban's Head. (UKHO © British Crown Copyright)

VIEW OF COWES.

| OPPOSITE | CHART OF SPITHEAD AND THE ISLE OF WIGHT BY WILLIAM HEATHER, 1797 | Following an apprenticeship to the engraver George Michell, a bookseller and stationer in Bond Street, Heather worked with John Hamilton Moore, chart publisher and navigation teacher, becoming a freeman of the Stationers' Company in 1789. He learned much through Moore, and met many of the navy's sailing masters, such as Joseph Dessiou, James Jameson (Nelson's sailing master) and Samuel Clements, master of the Royal Yacht. In 1793 he opened his own business in Leadenhall Street, where his firm remained for the next 85 years. Heather's 1797 catalogue lists 84 loose charts, including this one, which he dedicated to the Master Wardens and Elder Brethren of Trinity House. John Norrie, 12 years his junior, had joined him in 1796 and was already teaching navigation. He was to take over the business on Heather's early death at 46 and to prosper with his partner, George Wilson. Eventually, through a series of share transfers, the company continued, to become today the well-known chart and navigation aid suppliers Imray, Laurie, Norie and Wilson Ltd. (UKHO © British Crown Copyright)

| ABOVE | NAVIGATIONAL VIEW OF COWES, ISLE OF WIGHT, BY COMMANDER E W BROOKER, 1864 | This attractive navigational view of Cowes Harbour, with the Royal Yacht Club House identified, looks peaceful, if busy, with a mix of masted paddle steamers and sailing vessels anchored or sailing nearby. To the left, Ryde Pier can just be seen and the navigational note gives the mariner a visual point of reference to approach keeping clear of the Prince Consort Shoal.

Brooker's interesting survey career gives an indication of the sort of variety that some experienced in Victorian times with an Empire to map. Having served under Captain Owen Stanley in HMS *Rattlesnake* surveying the Torres Strait and around New Guinea, he was sailing master in HMS *Spitfire* in the Crimean War (1853–56), then surveying parts of Tasmania. He surveyed Spithead and around the Isle of Wight in 1864 and took command of HMS *Sylvia*, a screw-driven sloop, to survey for four years in Chinese and Korean waters. (UKHO © British Crown Copyright)

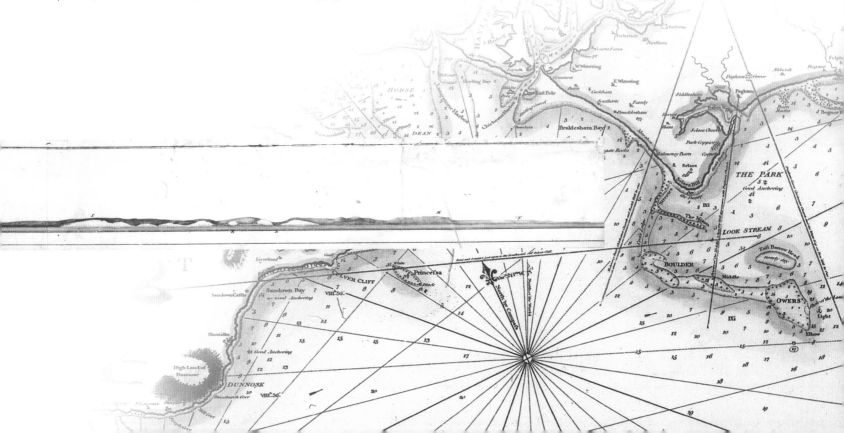

| ABOVE | MANUSCRIPT CHART OF LYME BAY, 1579 | Naive and attractive, this sixteenth-century chart features what must have been a significant harbour, Ottermouth Haven, complete with sailing instructions. It is taken from the Atlas of William Cecil, Lord Burghley, who was Elizabeth I's faithful chief advisor for 40 years. The coast is drawn around Lyme Bay from Weymouth to Dartmouth, with the principal ports and harbours marked. This stretch of coastline has one of the most complete geological time sequences through the Triassic, Jurassic and Cretaceous periods anywhere in the world, because the land slopes slowly towards the east exposing successively younger rocks to sea level. Looking carefully at the entrance to the River Otter you can see the curving breakwater sheltering some fishing boats; first built around 1300. (By permission of the British Library: ff.9v-10)

| BELOW | PLYMOUTH SOUND, 1697 | This vista of Plymouth Sound comes from a 'Survey and Description of the principal Harbours with their accomodations and conveniences for erecting, moaring, secureing and refitting the Navy Royall of England'. It describes the scene thus: 'Plymouth Sound and the River Hamouze and Catwater, from above the rising land above Mount Edgecombe, opposite Mount Wise, which shows St Nicholas Island as the principal guard to the New Dock and the ships in this harbour'. (By permission of the British Library: KINGS 43)

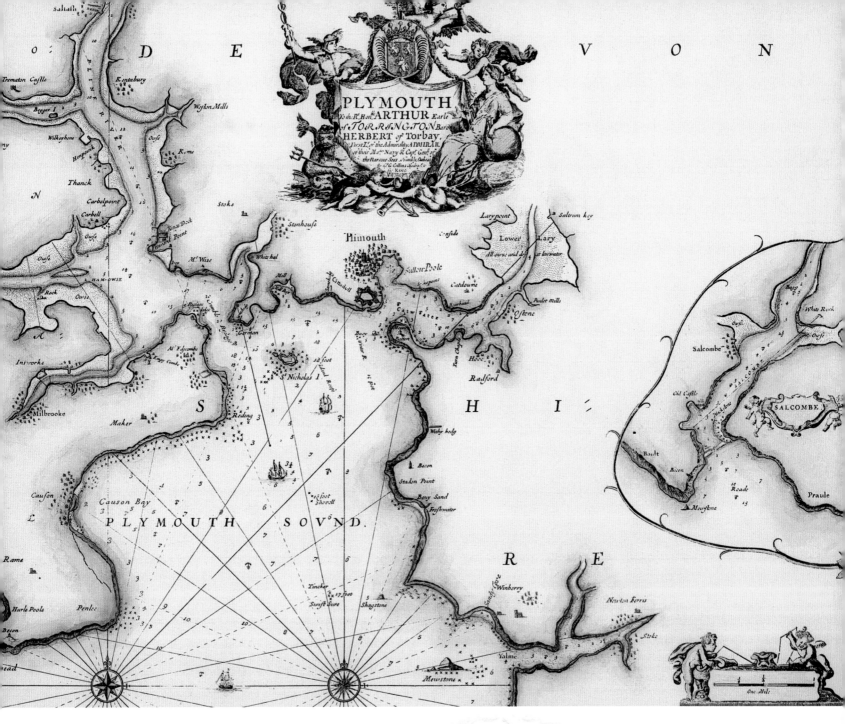

| CHART OF PLYMOUTH BY CAPTAIN GREENVILE COLLINS,

1693 | Collins' chart of Plymouth shows the Sound well before the breakwater was built making an already superb natural harbour in the drowned valleys of the Plym and Tamar into a defensive naval harbour and dockyard. The monks of nearby Plympton had patronised the harbour, which grew from a fishing village into a port in 1311 where wool and tin were exported and Bordeaux wines imported, but their influence didn't stop it becoming a haven for pirates. Many famous expeditions started out from here: Sir Humphrey Gilbert to colonise America in 1583, Sir Francis Drake on his circumnavigation in 1577, and the English fleet under Lord Howard of Effingham to attack the Spanish Armada in 1588. The dockyard at Devonport was built in 1689. (UKHO © British Crown Copyright)

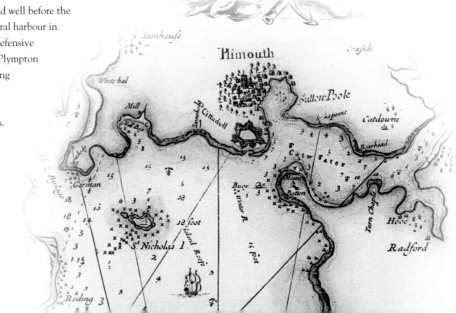

| HYDROGRAPHIC
OFFICE CHART
OF FALMOUTH,
PUBLISHED IN 1802,
FROM LIEUTENANT
MURDOCH
MACKENZIE'S SURVEY
OF 1781 | The sheer
professionalism of
Mackenzie's surveys
stands out on this chart.
Soundings are copious,
leading marks and clearing
bearings, to ensure a safe
passage into harbour, are
accurate and are taken
on readily identifiable
features ashore. There is an
abundance of navigational
information, such as the
best anchorages, nature
of the sea bottom, tidal
streams and high and low
water indications. Captain
Thomas Hurd, who became
Hydrographer in succession
to Dalrymple, was a highly
experienced hydrographer
and had spent nine years
surveying Bermuda, and
undertaking an important
survey off Brest in 1804.
He has added his own
remarks to pass on his
experience for the benefit
of navy ships of the
line. (Admiralty Library
Manuscript Collection:
Vf 2/28)

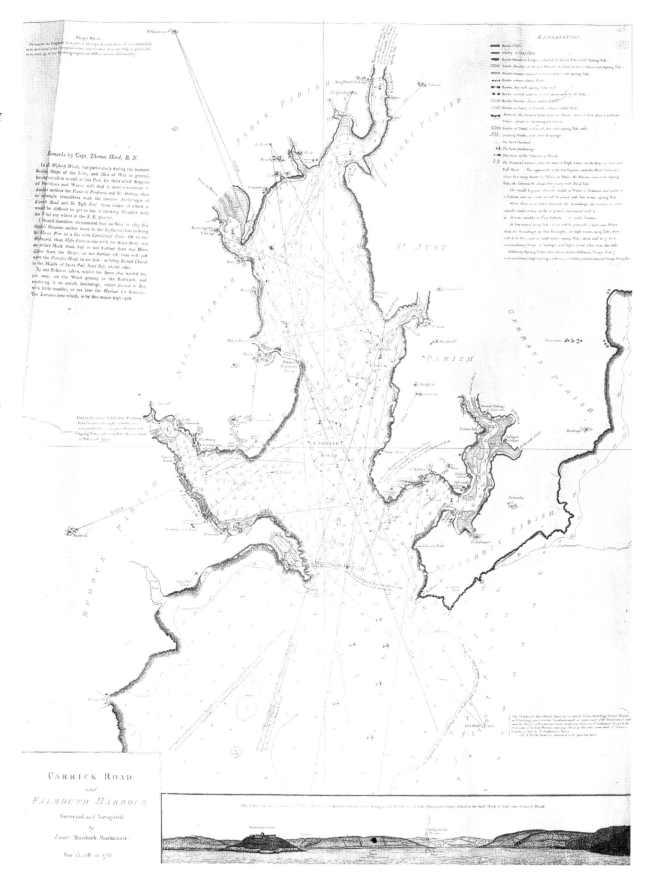

| A SURVEY OF THE SCILLY
ISLES BY GRAEME SPENCE,
1792 | The first Admiralty
chart published of the Scilly Isles
was drawn by Graeme Spence in
1792. Spence had taken over from
Lt Murdoch Mackenzie as chief
surveyor to the Admiralty in 1788,
and he had worked directly for
Trinity House in helping them to
site their new lightships, such as
the Owers in the Channel.

This is a stunning piece of
hydrographic surveying with 23
views of the indented, complex
coast of this island group battered
by the Atlantic. Lying about 30
miles off Land's End, with balmy
temperatures year-round, it is an
internationally important area with
large numbers of sea birds breeding
on the islands, including the red-
beaked puffin, and most notably
the European storm-petrel, with
possibly as many as 17,000 on the
archipelago. Over 400 species have
been recorded with new species
continually added. This total beats
any other single site in Europe,
being made up primarily of bird
vagrants. (UKHO © British
Crown Copyright)

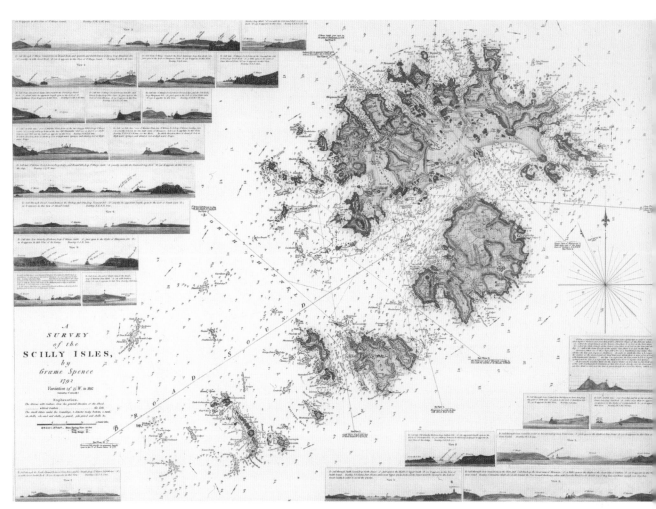

| PART OF THE SURVEY OF
ENGLAND'S SOUTHERN
COAST C. 1540 | Thomas
Cromwell ordered this survey of
the Cornish and Devon coasts
between Land's End and Exeter to
review the defences of Henry VIII's
realm against the threat of Spanish
or French attack and is one of the
earliest existing charts made for that
purpose. This section includes the
important naval base of Plymouth.
It shows, exaggerated, widened and
foreshortened from an invader's
viewpoint, where existing sea-forts
were positioned and, perhaps more
importantly, where coastal defences
were weak and additional forts
should be built, but it gives the
coastal panorama an extraordinary
appeal. (By permission of the British
Library: Cotton Augustus I.i.35)

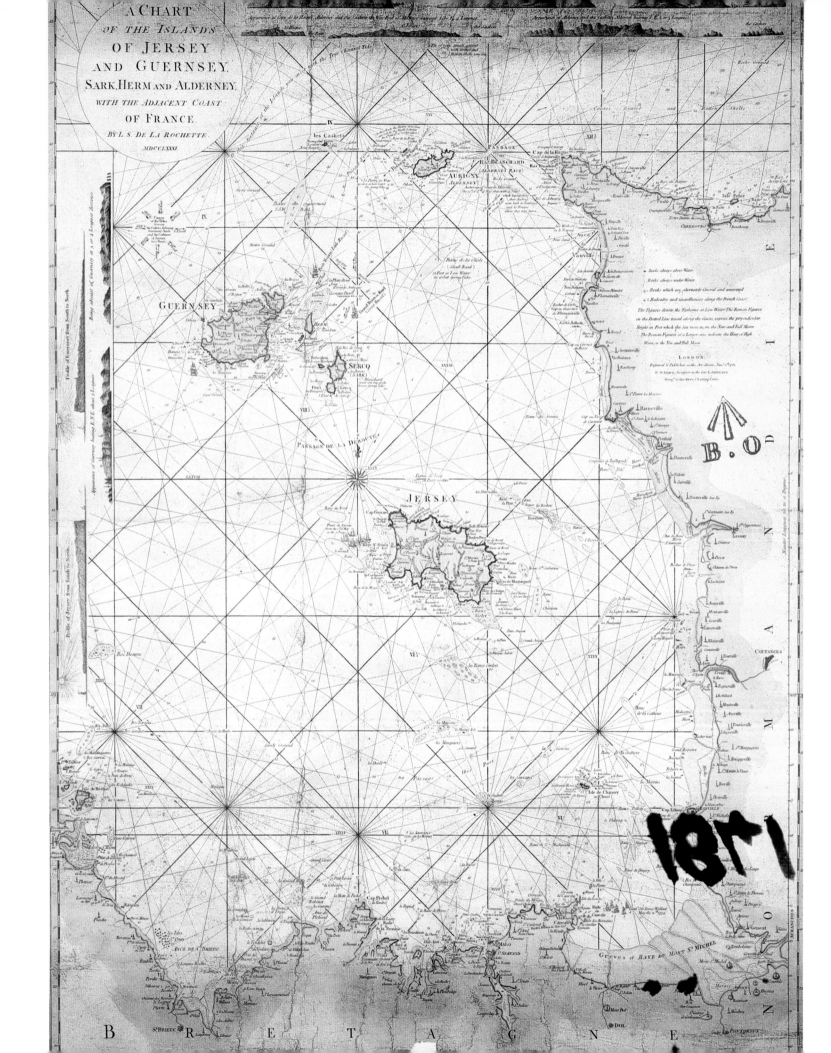

A CHART
OF THE ISLANDS
OF JERSEY
AND GUERNSEY,
SARK, HERM AND ALDERNEY,
WITH THE ADJACENT COAST
OF FRANCE
BY L. S. DE LA ROCHETTE.
MDCCLXXXI

| OPPOSITE | CHART OF THE CHANNEL ISLANDS BY LOUIS STANISLAS D'ARCY DE LA ROCHETTE, 1781 | This chart shows all the Channel Islands framed by the French coast. It was produced by the cartographer Louis Stanislas D'Arcy de la Rochette, who was associated with the publisher William Faden in London. It has a number of coastal views and tidal information, with latitude and longitude, but also the 16 graticule points (not on the land) around a central compass rose giving a plotting grid or framework as was used on earlier charts, but dropped with the Admiralty charts from the early nineteenth century. (The National Archives {PRO}: MPH1/566)

| LEFT | EIGHTEENTH-CENTURY VIEWS OF GUERNSEY, JERSEY AND ALDERNEY | The Channel Islands were politically linked to Brittany until 933 when they were seized and annexed to Normandy. In 1204, when Normandy broke away, they remained with England. Always exposed to attack from the French during the many wars over the centuries, the islanders needed to build a number of forts and castles for protection, for example, Castle Cornet in Guernsey and Elizabeth Castle in Jersey.

These views, engraved by W H Toms after Captain Clement Lemprière, show the three largest of the Channel Islands. Guernsey and Jersey both show the dominant positions of the castles at the entrance to the harbours; the view of Alderney includes Guernsey 'at 7 leagues distant' (shown at indicator 10) and Normandy on the horizon. Eight views were published by John Tinngy in London in 1731 and are some of the earliest printed views of the islands. (Admiralty Library Manuscript Collection: {from top} Vz 11/15, Vz 11/16, Vz 11/12)

ST. GEORGES CHANNEL

PART OF THE IRIS[H]

PART OF THE COUNTY OF

PEMBROKE

A
Chart of the Coast
of
WALES
in St. George's Channel,
drawn from an Actual Survey now
lying at the Admiralty Office, and
made between the Years 1737 & 1744,
by the Order and Encouragement
of the Lords of the Admiralty.
By Lewis Morris.
By Comparing this Chart with all that
have been done before, it will be found
that there are here laid down, several
Banks, Overfalls, sunken rocks & other Material
discoveries of dangers, w. hitherto have been known
only to a few Coasters, the Principal of which are the
Coal rock, y Garreg goch hen, several banks about
Bardsey, also Sarn Badrig, The Auger bank,
Porgus bank &c. the knowledge of which & this
publication cannot but be of the Utmost
Consequence to trade & Navigation.

Part of the County of CARDIGAN

PART OF
MERIONETH SHIRE

Part of the County of CAERNAR[VON]

Compass Course for the Year. 1748
The True Meridian

A Scale of Leagues

5   10   15

Note. The principal Harbours, Roads, and sounds included here, are to be had in Plans at Large, in a
Volume done by the Author hereof; By the help of which, together with this Chart, any Sailor who
understands the use of Sea Draughts, by bringing the meridians of that and this in the same position may
carry his vessel into a safe road, or a Harbour.

Publish'd by the Author according to Act of Parliament Sept. 30. 1748.

CHAPTER IV

THE WEST COAST OF
ENGLAND
& WALES

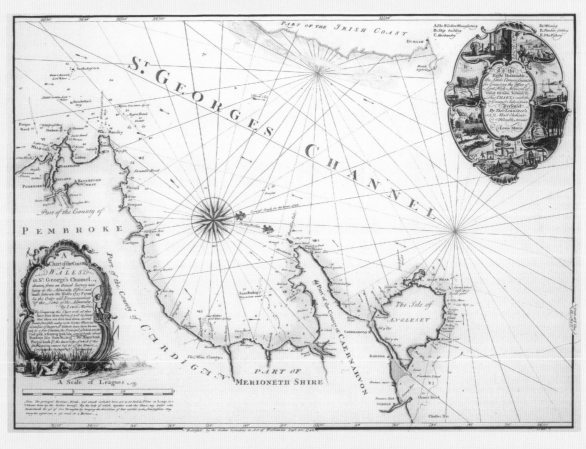

| LEFT DETAIL & ABOVE | CHART OF ST GEORGE'S CHANNEL AND WALES BY LEWIS MORRIS, 1748 | Lewis Morris came from a well-known Welsh family, the Morrisiad Môn (The Morrises of Anglesey). His marine survey of the Welsh coast, undertaken with very little official support, was a supreme prioneering achievement, especially for a self-taught hydrographer. It is for this survey that he is now recognised as one of the eminent British cartographers. The charts were published privately in September 1748. All of them were a significant improvement on earlier ones and provided a wealth of additional information on tidal streams, anchorages and hazards. These works preceded improved charts based on the Admiralty's own surveys by about 70 years. (UKHO © British Crown Copyright)

THE west coast of England has two of the Isles' largest ports – Bristol and Liverpool, and Wales has one of the most important – Milford Haven. Unlike the south coast where every river outlet was competing for the Channel business, there are fewer harbours.

The hard granite of Land's End changes to the greenstone of Cape Cornwall, Gurnards Head and Zennor Head and the island of St Ives, a typical Cornish fishing village. It has had to learn to cater for the tourist and surfer, as the unspoilt Atlantic rollers break along these shores providing ideal surf into such bays as Perran Bay, named after the Irish missionary Saint Piran, who used the oldest chapel in the south-west dating from the seventh century, Watergate Bay and Port Isaac Bay.

The town of Newquay benefited, as did Padstow, from the nineteenth-century rail-head. The pilchard industry was strong here and the lookout houses still stand, such as that on Towan Head where the 'huer' could see the red pilchard shoal in the sea below and cry out to direct the fishermen with their long seine net to entrap the fish on to the shore line – the original 'hue and cry'.

When the Camel river silted up trade moved from Wadebridge to Padstow, but today the river forms a fine estuary to sail from. Port Isaac remains unspoilt with narrow medieval streets and fishermen's cottages, and Tintagel, a purported birthplace of King Arthur rivals it. These pretty north-Cornish villages continue up the coast with Boscastle, tragically inundated in 2004, as was Lynmouth, in Devon, in 1953. During a storm in 1899 in which they were unable to launch the lifeboat, the people of Lynmouth took it over hills and along tracks to launch it from Porlock 13 miles east and 11 hours away in order to save the Forrest Hall. There is a good view of Lundy Island, the old lair for pirates and smugglers, from Hartland Point, known to the Romans as the Promontory of Hercules where Clovelly fishing village nestles further into Bideford Bay.

Appledore is placed at the entrance from Bideford Bay into the estuary mouth of the Rivers Torridge and Taw, draining Dartmoor to the north with the towns of Bideford and Barnstaple straddling them. There are few harbours along the coast north of Exmoor, whose waters drain south along the River Exe to the English Channel at Exmouth, so local cargo was taken to Ilfracombe, which had 70 indigenous ships and a flourishing shipyard during the nineteenth century; Watchet, from where iron mined in the Brendon Hills was exported, or Minehead, used by eighteenth-century traders with woollen yarn from Ireland. By now the land is falling away to low-lying flat land bounded to the north by the Mendip Hills.

The constricting shape of the Severn Estuary creates a phenomenon known as the Severn Bore, as the tide flows in at a speed of over 10 knots up as high as Gloucester or Tewkesbury some 20 miles upstream, which caused problems for those attempting a river crossing before the first suspension bridge was completed in 1966.

Bristol's history as a major port goes back to Saxon times. It traded with Ireland, taking indigenous cloth to Gascony, Portugal and Spain, and importing wines on the return voyage. The Avon Gorge provided a natural defence, but the winding River Avon (Afon is Welsh for river) presented a navigational problem, too such an extent that in the Middle Ages ships had to be towed and in 1662 the City Corporation set a limit of 60 tons, as bigger ships grounded. However, the diarist Celia Fiennes was still able to write in 1696: 'the town is a very great trading city as most in England, and is esteemed the largest next to London'. In 1712 a wet dock was built where the Romans had built a harbour at Sea Mills, but it lacked a road connection with the city. A new wet dock built at Hotwells in 1768 took over but the restriction of Horseshoe Bend prevented ships longer than 300 feet from entering.

Losing trade to Liverpool provided the incentive to extend the docks over a 70-acre area, with a lock giving access to a new basin – Cumberland Basin – diverting the River Avon along a specially dug channel, known as the New Cut. Another canal was dug from the dam to the River Avon to give access for the laden barges upstream to Bath. Trade with North America re-invigorated the harbour, and Bristol did well out of the slave trade, exploiting the triangle of trade first to Africa with iron and firearms, to the Caribbean with slaves, and back with sugar. But the abolition of the slave trade in 1807, and the emancipation of the slaves themselves in 1833, brought about the collapse of the sugar trade as plantations in Jamaica were abandoned. In 1830, 63 per cent of Bristol's trade was with the West Indies; by 1871 it was down to 29 per cent, and by 1890, is was zero.

Bristol has consistently responded to new opportunities, building new docks at Avonmouth, while today the port of Bristol has been re-developed with dock-side housing and leisure attractions, including the SS *Great Britain*, the first screw-propelled, ocean-going ship, which was built and launched in Bristol in 1843.

Looking into Wales, the Normans were easily able to advance along the southern coastal regions, building castles as they progressed west to control the local area. The Welsh re-settled into the hills and mountains of the interior, north of the cultural divide known as the Landsker. The Flemish, economic migrants of the fifteenth century, were offered land by Henry VII and settled as far west as Pembrokeshire building their own style of house. The nineteenth-century railway allowed the coal mining activities to expand with coal being brought from the valleys to the ports of Barry, Newport and Cardiff.

| AVON GORGE WITH CLIFTON SUSPENSION BRIDGE BY W H BARTLETT | A view of Avon Gorge with Brunel's suspension bridge, completed in 1864, showing the 'tortuous River Avon', which ships had to negotiate to get to Bristol Docks. (By permission of the British Library: 1503/320 Vol. II.

The Normans built a castle at Newport in the thirteenth century. It suffered in the Civil War in 1648, but grew rapidly in the early nineteenth century with the completion of the Monmouth and Brecon Canals.

Cardiff, the capital of Wales, was a Roman town initially, and enlarged by the Normans. The Welsh burned it in 1185, and again under Owen Glyndwr in 1404. Swansea, originally named Swein's Eye after the Viking King, Swein Forkbeard of Denmark, who was briefly King of England in 1013–14 and raided this coast, similarly developed around a Norman castle, and prospered as the centre for the Gower peninsula, now a rich and pleasant contrast of peace and beauty compared to the industrialised south Welsh coast. Its strategic position at the mouth of the River Tawe gave it the opportunity to expand hugely with the coal trade.

Pembrokeshire has some of the finest natural coasts to be found anywhere in Britain, and the Pembrokeshire Coast National Park was created in recognition of this in 1952. The English so colonised it in the Middle Ages that it still known as 'little England beyond Wales'. And Tenby remains a popular resort with fine Georgian terrace houses surrounded by the original Norman town walls, although the Norman castle was shattered by Oliver Cromwell's army during the Civil War. Then the plague of 1650-51, as with many towns, killed half the population. It has a fine harbour and golden sandy beaches either side, making it a natural holiday destination for families since Georgian times. Fortunately for the tourist industry, conventions have changed since the start of the upsurge in sea bathing when the local Victorians disapprovingly reported the inclination to adopt the 'naughty French custom of mixed bathing'.

The coastal paths are wonderful to walk with great geological diversity carved by the elements into the varying hardness of successive folded layers of limestone, millstone grit and red sandstone. These have left us amazing rock structures, such as the

| SOUTH STACK LIGHTHOUSE, HOLYHEAD, BY W H BARTLETT
1842 | A hundred feet separates the tiny islet of South Stack Rock from
Holyhead Island, but the sea surges through restlessly and relentlessly. The
whole coastline is of sheer granite rising to 160 feet, and the lighthouse was
built in 1809, with originally a hemp bridge to slide stores across in a basket,
which was replaced by the iron bridge in the illustration in 1828. (By permission
of the British Library: 1502/320 Vol. II)

Green Bridge of Wales and the Elegug Stacks, home to puffins
and choughs, cormorants and kittiwakes, with the offshore
islands of Skokholm and Skomer providing homes for colonies of
seabirds and the Atlantic grey seals.

The natural deep-water harbour of Milford Haven is the
berth for thousands of private sailing craft, but it is also one of
the most important ports for oil tankers who unload their crude
straight to the refineries.

Pembroke, with the nineteenth-century naval base along the
reach, is also a Norman town with its castle both dominating the
town and in very much the same shape as when built in 1093. The
town was an important medieval seaport until Haverfordwest,

well up the River Cleddau, took the trade, principally coal, wool
and fish.

The old town of Fishguard, again of Norman foundation,
has an unspoilt charm. In consequence, it was chosen as the
archetypal Welsh village for the film version of the Dylan
Thomas's *Under Milk Wood* (1972) with Richard Burton and
Elizabeth Taylor, posing as the village of Llareggub. Here, too,
the American hero of Independence, John Paul Jones, took a
merchant ship and fired off a couple of broadsides at the town,
and the French in 1797 actually invaded, the last invasion of
the British Isles. It came to nought as the locals didn't rise up
in support and march on Chester and Liverpool, and the 1400
strong force, who apparently mistook the red dresses of the Welsh
women to be English redcoats, was easily defeated.

Cardigan stands at the mouth of the River Teifi around the
coast from Dinas Head, which stands out into Cardigan Bay. This
old town, again with a Norman castle built during Henry I's reign,
was the main medieval port until Aberystwyth grew in response
to the interest in Welsh slate quarried around Machynlleth and

lead mines. Aberystwyth is well positioned at the mouth of two rivers Ystwyth and Rheidol. Following his successful invasion of Wales that began in 1277, Edward I began a great castle-building scheme. Edmund, Earl of Lancaster and Edward's brother, built the castle in 1277, which was reduced by Cromwell's forces in 1647. Visit Harlech Castle today, built as part of Edward I's Welsh containment policy, and it is hard to conceive that this was a port to keep the castle supplied from the sea during a siege, as it is now cut off by a pebble spit that has pushed the sea away. Porthmadog was developed by reclaiming the mud-flats to take the railways that brought the Snowdonian slate, which has roofed innumerable Victorian houses, to the quay side.

The architect, Sir Clough Williams-Elllis, undeterred by the climate, eccentrically created Portmeirion as an eighteenth-century Mediterranen port with Italian buildings. A few miles along the dramatic cliff coast of the Lleyn Peninsula Edward I built another castle at Criccieth to control Tremadog Bay and the coast road. It was burnt during Owen Glyndwr's rebellion in 1404, and had to wait for twentieth-century tourism to revive it.

Built by Edward I to control the south-western end of the Menai Strait that runs between Wales and Anglesey, the castle at Caernarfon served as the administrative centre for North Wales, and became a significant port for shipping out the Snowdonian slate. The King built another castle at Beaumaris on the Anglesey shore at the northern end of the strait, and the adjacent seaport harboured the herring fleet. There are a number of Holy Islands around the British shores. The one by Anglesey has the ferry port of Holyhead and the striking South Stack lighthouse adjacent, warning of the high cliffs and rocky shores, and there is evidence of significant bronze-age settlements.

Edward built yet another castle at Conwy in 1283, on a spur of land between the River Conwy to the east and the Gyffin to the south, where Telford's suspension bridge takes cars across between Colwyn Bay and Bangor.

The River Dee feeds into its own estuary through the town of Chester, sited by the Romans in AD 79 as a fortress to suppress the Welsh on a sandstone outcrop in a loop of the river at the lowest fordable stretch, which formed a natural harbour. The Roman walls still stand today, along with the amphitheatre. The city was sufficiently important that the cathedral was built in 1093 and an earl appointed, although the line died out in 1237 and the Prince of Wales holds the title. However, the Dee started to silt up, and by the fifteenth century merchant ships had to anchor 12 miles downstream, but during the Industrial Revolution a network of canals and railways were constructed.

Liverpool on the mouth of the River Mersey was one of Britain's greatest seaports, and took over from Chester as the Dee silted up. It had good communication with North America and Ireland and was the main port of departure for emigrants leaving to begin a new life in America. In 1871 the Bank Holiday Act was passed and for the first time workers from the mills, pits and foundries were able to take a weekend break. Blackpool took advantage of this and 20 northern town mayors attended the foundation ceremony for the Blackpool Tower, a 519 feet tall, half-size replica of the Eiffel Tower.

The dramatic inrush of tidal waters, with a range of 30 feet, into the 120 square miles of sand and mud flats that are Morecambe Bay gives an environment that supports a large cockle and mussel population off which around a quarter of a million waders live. An industry of collecting them has grown up sometimes with tragic results if these tides are not understood. In Norman times 'sand guides' would help travellers to take the short cut to Cumbria, and the 'Queen's Guides to the Sands' still exist, marking the safe path with laurel bushes pushed into the sand. But many carriages and lives have been lost in the quicksands around Black Scar. Morecambe itself developed as a tourist town, helped by the arrival of the railway in 1853.

Barrow-in-Furness was a considered Victorian development in response to the Industrial Age. Before the 1850s there was nothing more than a village and jetties for small coasters to load up the locally mined iron ore, and of course the beautiful Cistercian Abbey of Furness built in 1123 and the second largest in England, now a romantic ruin. A population explosion to 30,000 to work the blast furnaces by 1872 had doubled again by 1900, and for a time Barrow was the biggest steel and iron producer in the world, but today the steel works have closed. Barrow then developed into an important shipbuilding port, with many Royal Navy ships launched there.

On past the nuclear power station of Sellafield, built along the low coast, and accused of pollution along with so much industry further up that coast, into the Irish Sea, you come to the next significant natural feature, St Bees Head, with cliffs dominating sandy beaches and the port of Whitehaven sheltering to the north-east. In the eighteenth century it was on a par with Liverpool and Bristol exporting coal and manufactured goods to America, and importing tobacco, until, lacking the deep water necessary for the ever-growing tonnage of ships, the trade was lost to Glasgow. This was a family concern, built up by Sir John Lowther, and similarly Workington and Maryport were developed by, respectively, the Curwen and Senhouse families, initially trading coal from their estates and then producing iron and steel, and shipbuilding until commercial forces ran them down. These ports face across the Solway Firth to Scotland, which we look at in Chapter VI.

This plan comes from the collection of the Elizabethan antiquary, Sir Robert Cotton, who died in 1631, and is described as a 'posthumous founder' of the British Library. By 'gift and by stealth' he collected one of the earliest map collections in Europe, which reflects the mapping techniques and the preoccupations and working methods of Tudor and early Stuart administrators at a time when the needs of national defence were paramount. (By permission of the British Library: Cotton Augustus I.i.17)

This view of Hartland Quay, with Lundy Island on the horizon, provides an interesting snapshot of life by the coast with local fishing smacks running for shelter. The pier was built in the sixteenth century with a stone base of 40 feet, and took in lead, coal, slate and lime for the farmland's thin soil. The fishermen would also string a net across the mouth and could catch 1000 mullet on the ebb tide. After continuous erosion by the sea it was finally demolished by a storm in 1887: not without good reason is this coast – battered by up to 80-foot high Atlantic waves – known as the Iron Coast.

William Daniell was born in Kingston-upon-Thames, Surrey, the son of a bricklayer. He was trained to paint by his uncle, Thomas, who became a Royal Academician, as did William in 1821. Amongst other works, William published a series of stunning views of the British Isles in his book A Voyage Around Great Britain 1814 to 1825 in which this view is included. (By kind permission of Mark Myers © Hartland Quay Museum)

| PLAN OF CARDIFF, C. 1650 | The French were always on the on the lookout for an opportunity to invade the British Isles, and this plan is from a collection of French plans of the fortifications of towns and ports in England, the Netherlands and Germany dating to about 1650.

The plan shows Cardiff Castle, built in 1091 by Robert Fitzhamon, where the River Taff meanders to the Bristol Channel, and a settlement grew up around it, to be razed by Owen Glyndwr in 1404. During Elizabethan times it was a lair for pirates and by the eighteenth century it was a quiet town of 1500 residents. The Bute family saw the opportunities of the Industrial Revolution, built a canal joining Cardiff with Merthyr Tydfil and the city's first dock in 1839. By 1913 it was the biggest coal-exporting port in the world with over 13,000,000 tons shipped out. Today its function is more historic and administrative as the capital city of Wales. (By permission of the British Library: ADD.11564)

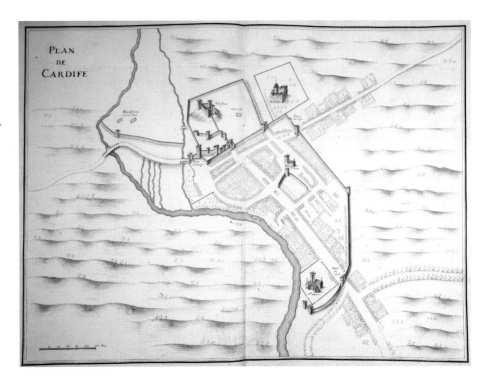

| CHART OF CARDIFF BY LIEUTENANT HENRY DENHAM, PUBLISHED IN 1832 | To cope with the increased shipping, the Butes built docks, starting with the Bute West Dock in 1835, the East Dock in 1855, then Roath Basin in 1874, and, with demand for coal and steel still growing, Roath Dock in 1877 and the Queen Alexandra Dock in 1907, with the consequent explosion of workers and housing adjacent, attracting over 50 nationalities into 'Tiger Bay'. Lieutenant Denham's chart of 1832 pre-dates all of the dockland development, merely showing the Bute Ship Canal and Dock, but with a wealth of navigational detail that became the hallmark of the Admiralty chart. (UKHO © British Crown Copyright)

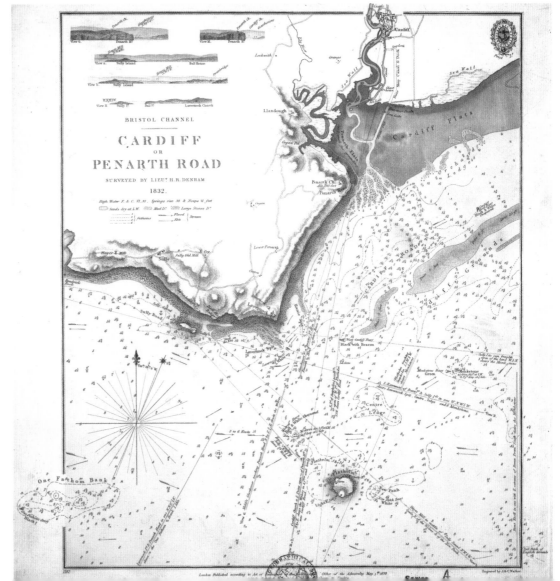

| CHART OF TENBY APPROACHES BY LEWIS MORRIS, 1748 | At Tenby the Normans built a castle on top of the hill overlooking a harbour below. They built the town enclosed by walls that are still very largely intact today. Tenby, with Milford and Carmarthen, were the prime ports, while Norman castles were built as part of a chain at Haverfordwest, Manorbier and Pembroke. In the fourteenth century, while Haverfordwest encouraged commercial relations with Ireland to trade wool and hides, exempted from port dues, Tenby secured a grant from Edward III in 1328 to build a breakwater, and became one of the principal herring ports in Wales. From the early fourteenth century to early sixteenth century ships were bringing wine and salt from France, Spain and Portugal; twice as many ships came to Tenby as to Bristol, according to a 1566 report by the Commission to Suppress Piracy, handling half the county's foreign trade. By 1662 between a quarter and one third of Pembrokeshire coal was handled through the harbour, while ale was transported to Bristol, London, Barnstaple, Dartmouth, Exeter, Bideford, Falmouth, the Scillies, Bridgwater, Liverpool, Chester and Abertaw.

This was one of the charts of the survey Lewis made of St George's Channel and the Pembrokeshire coast. His notes on the tides and tidal streams were a useful addition.

Also shown is the cover to his book of charts. It includes illustrations of the cross-staff and the backstaff, used by navigators to measure the altitude of the sun and stars. The commercial message of | the contrasting images between the shipwreck and the safe arrival into port is self-apparent! (By courtesy of the Dean and Chapter of Westminster)

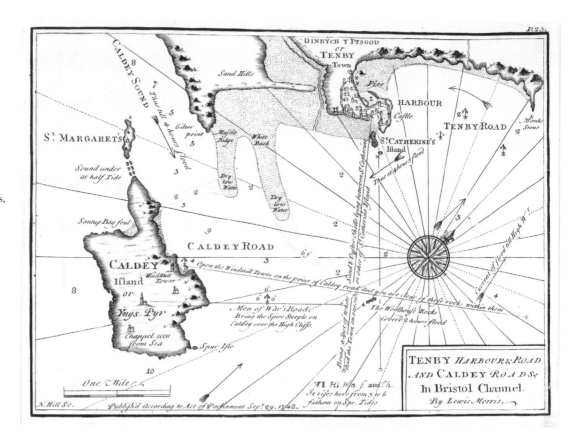

| RIGHT | CHART OF HOLYHEAD BY CAPTAIN
WILLIAM BLIGH, 1801 | Captain Bligh is mostly
remembered by posterity as the captain of the mutinous
HMS Bounty. But history could be kinder, because
without this mutiny he would be celebrated as an
outstanding navigator, surveyor and wartime sea captain,
achieved during a full naval career culminating in the
position of Vice-Admiral. In December 1800, he was
ordered, 'at the desire of His Excellency Marquis
Cornwallis, Lord Lieutenant of Ireland by the Right
Honourable the Lords Commissioners of the Admiralty
in Great Britain' to survey the bay of Dublin. This was
to facilitate the passage of the packet ferries from Dublin
to Holyhead. He then went to Holyhead to sketch the
survey that is reproduced here in January 1801. It is a
simple, but accurate survey, which has been signed by
Bligh, although it is not as detailed as more complete
surveys that would take much longer. (UKHO © British
Crown Copyright)

| BELOW | MILFORD HAVEN BY CAPTAIN
GEORGE WATSON, 1765 | This chart shows the
superb, natural deep-water harbour of Milford Haven and
the River Cleddau up to Lawrenny, including the Norman
keep at Benton and the site of the later nearby Royal
Naval Dockyard of Pembroke Dock, where over 250
Royal Navy ships were built, including six Royal Yachts,
between 1815 and 1922.

Captain Watson used colour to clarify this chart:
green to show the navigable fairway, and yellow for the
banks that dry at low tide. (Admiralty Library Manuscript
Collection: Vz 11/27)

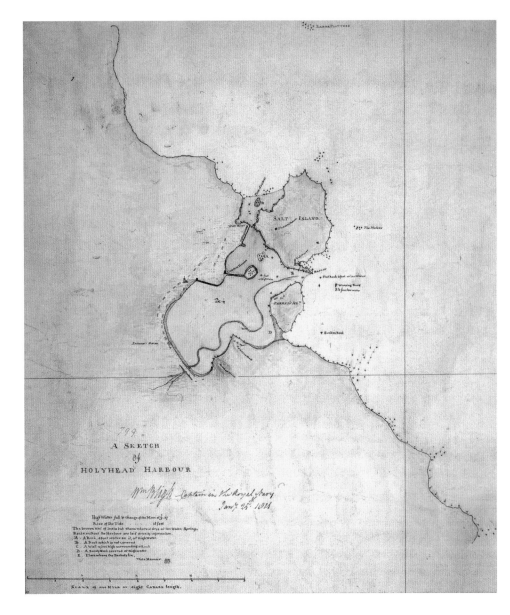

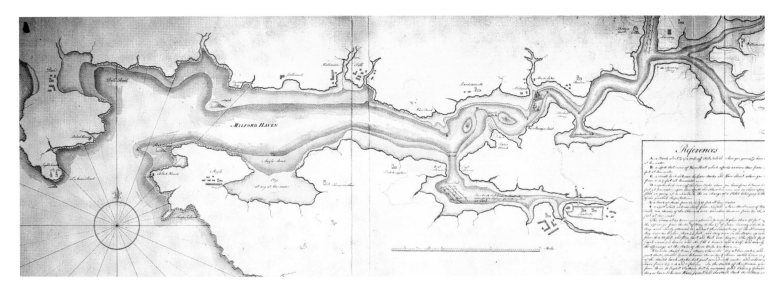

| PLAN OF THE CITY AND CASTLE OF CHESTER BY ALEXANDER DE LAVAUX, 1745 |

It is hard to believe today that Chester was a thriving port in medieval times, the largest in the north-west, before the River Dee silted up, with an immense Roman harbour, now the famous Roodeye Racecourse, the oldest in Britain (and where the horses race anti-clockwise). James Boswell, Dr Samuel Johnson's biographer, declared: 'Chester pleases my fancy more than any town I saw', and certainly it has much to offer the visitor, from the old port and the 1072 cathedral of St Wereberg, to the amphitheatre that provided amusement for the legions stationed in the headquarters for the north.

De Lavaux published two maps of Chester in 1745, one a large-scale plan of the castle, which proved his credentials as a military engineer, and this one of the city. It has two elaborate cartouches, one with Chester's coat of arms and the other the coat of arms of the Lord Lieutenant of Cheshire, George the Earl of Cholmondeley. (UKHO © British Crown Copyright)

| CHART OF THE ISLE OF MAN, BY CAPTAIN GREENVILE COLLINS,
1693 | The Isle of Man sits in the Irish Sea virtually equidistant from England,
Ireland, Scotland and Wales. As a British Crown dependency, it is an independent
country within the British Commonwealth and has its own Parliament, the
Tynewald, running its affairs, while relying on the United Kingdom for defence.
For some centuries it was a pirates' haven. It was a part of the Norwegian
Kingdom until the thirteenth century, from which time it was controlled by
Scotland, coming under British control from the fourteenth century and sold to
the British crown by the Duke of Atholl for £70,000 in 1765. Its independence
enables it to run its financial affairs free of British Government control. The
origin of the name is obscure, and goes back in antiquity, but could be from the
Irish, meaning 'linked to water' or 'at the water's edge'. There is a movement for
maintaining the Manx language and the Island's ancient symbol, the Triskelion, is
said to relate to the Island's motto '*Quocunque Jeceris Stabit*' – 'Withersoever you
throw it, it will stand'.

The chart by Collins was published in 1693 in his *Great Britain's Coasting Pilot*
and with latitude only, and North orientated to the right, gives the island's main
features, anchorages, rocks, shoals and soundings, and a little tidal information.
It was engraved by Hermann Moll, who sold navigational globes to the mariner in
London. (UKHO © British Crown Copyright)

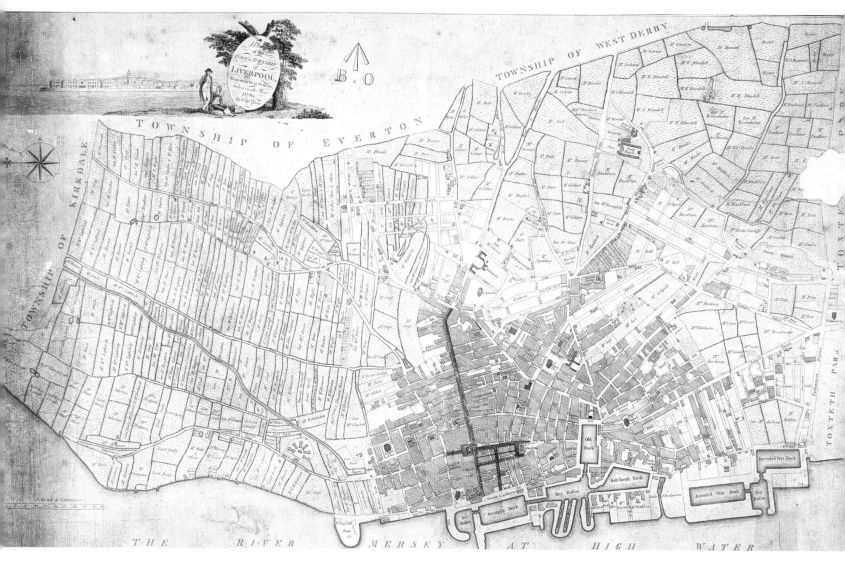

| LIVERPOOL DOCKS, 1785 | Liverpool is one of Britain's greatest ports. This plan shows the docks, and proposed new docks, in 1785; fields with owners' or occupiers' names; mills, public buildings and places of worship. The adjoining towns are all shown, along with the Leeds to Liverpool Canal and a view, set in the cartouche, of the town from across the Mersey in 1785.

Originally colonised by Norsemen, the city's name Hlitharpollr meant 'pool of the slopes'. Liverpool was granted a charter by Henry III in 1229 to form a guild of merchants, but didn't flourish until the merchants discovered the profitable slave trade in the eighteenth century. The first slaver of 60 tons sailed in 1709 with 15 slaves across the Atlantic to sell them in the West Indies. By 1809, 185 slave ships operated carrying 49,213 slaves, returning with a cargo of rum and sugar, and

Liverpool became bigger than Bristol. It was a hub for privateering during the Seven Years War and the American War of Independence, with, for example in 1778, 120 privateers being fitted out in the port. After the war trade developed hugely with America and raw cotton was brought in to feed the massive cotton industry of Lancashire. It was commercially natural to extend the port to cater for the growing ocean liner traffic crossing to the Americas, and many Irish and European emigrants sailed from there and also from the new port at Birkenhead, across the Mersey.

The successful campaign against the German U-boats during the Second World War was organised from the headquarters of the Western Approaches Command of the Royal Navy in Liverpool. (The National Archives {PRO}: MPH1/351)

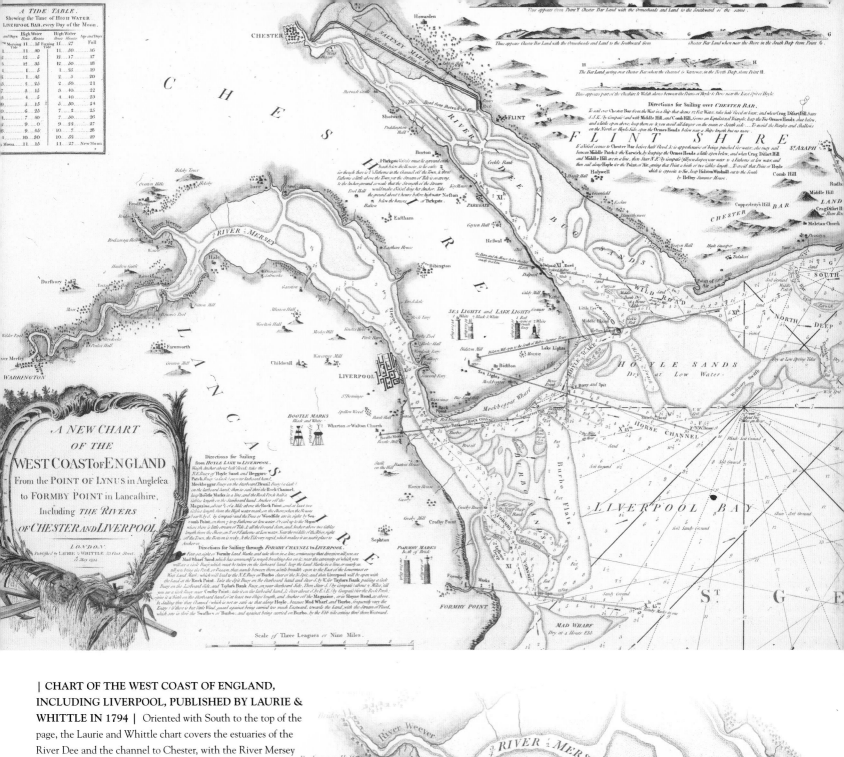

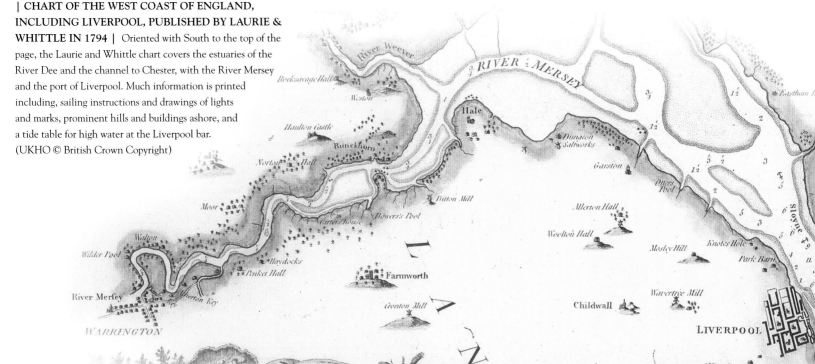

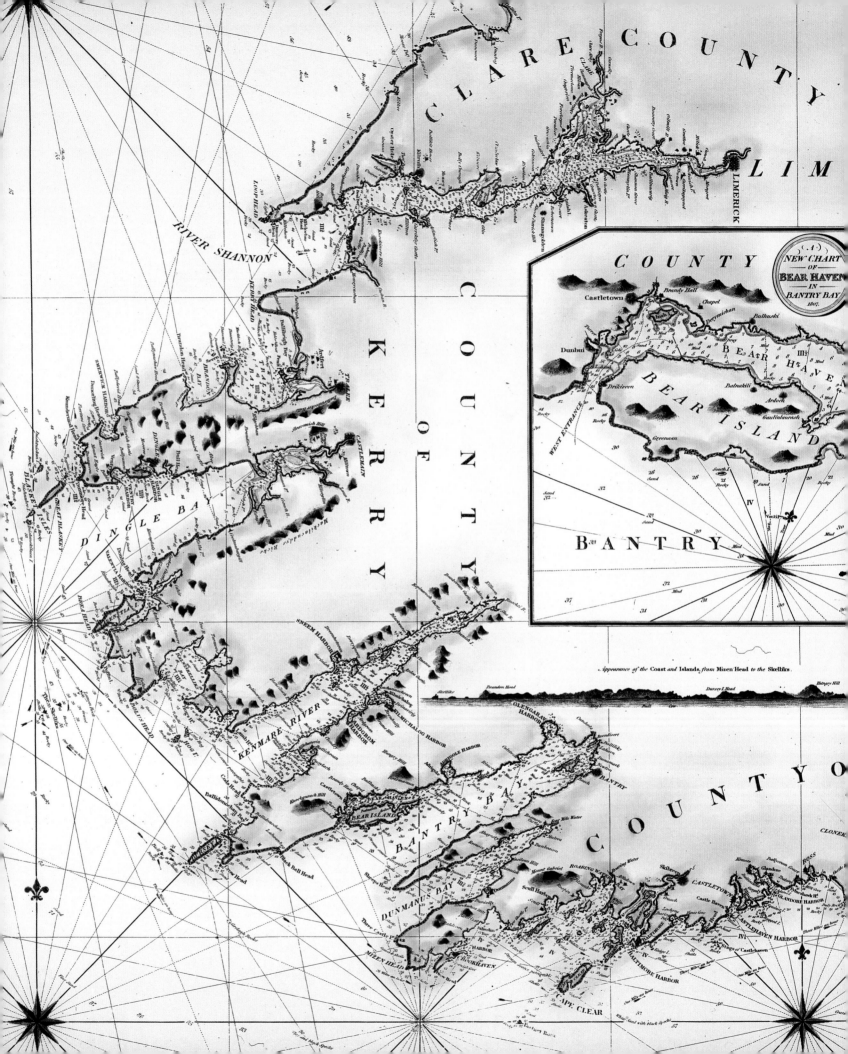

CLARE COUNTY

LIM

LIMERICK

RIVER SHANNON

LOOP HEAD

KERRY HEAD

KERRY

COUNTY

OF

KERRY

BLASKET ISLES

GREAT BLASKET

DINGLE BAY

DINGLE

VALENTIA

SNEEM HARBOR

KENMARE RIVER

BEAR ISLAND

DURSEY

Crow Head

Black Ball Head

BANTRY BAY

Sheeps Head

DUNMANUS BAY

MIZEN HEAD

CROOKHAVEN

CAPE CLEAR

GLENGARRY HARBOR

BANTRY

BALTIMORE HARBOR

Mount Gabriel

Scull Harbor

CASTLETOWN

Castle Haven

ROSS

GLANDORE HARBOR

CASTLEHAVEN HARBOR

COUNTY O

CLONEK

New Chart of Bear Haven in Bantry Bay (inset)

A NEW CHART OF BEAR HAVEN IN BANTRY BAY. 1807.

COUNTY

Castletown

Brandy Hall

Chapel

Dunbui

Drikiveen

BEAR HAVEN

BEAR ISLAND

Greenaan

Balnakili

Ardoch

Gaulinlaurash

WEST ENTRANCE

South I.

BANTRY

Appearance of the Coast and Islands, from Mizen Head to the Skelliks.

Skelliks Brandon Head Dursey I. Head Ridney Hill

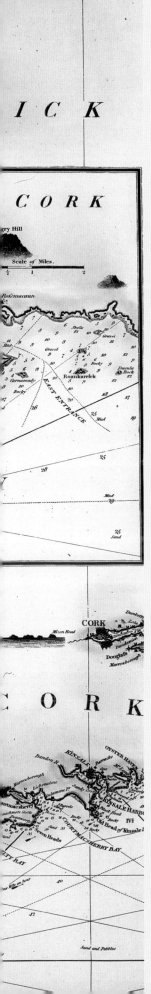

CHAPTER V

EIRE
& NORTHERN IRELAND

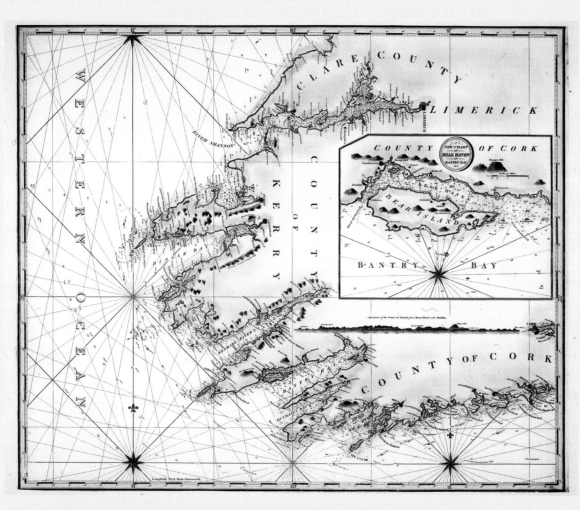

| LEFT DETAIL & ABOVE | CHART OF THE COASTLINE FROM OLD HEAD OF KINSALE TO DONEGAL POINT BY WILLIAM HEATHER, 1807 | At the south-west corner of Ireland there are five peninsulas that jut aggressively but with great attraction into the Atlantic. Mizen Head is the most southerly peninsula; Sheep's Head is to the south-east of Bantry Bay. The Beara Peninsula, named after a Spanish princess who married an Irish chieftain, and the Iveragh Peninsula confine the Kenmare river and estuary. The fifth peninsula is Dingle, with Ireland's second highest peak, Mount Brandon at 951 metres, to the north. (UKHO © British Crown Copyright)

AS the most westerly island of the British Isles (in a geographical sense) Ireland gets more rain first, justifiably giving her the oft-used other name of The Emerald Isle. The saucer shaped geology combines relatively high surrounding mountains, the highest being Carrauntohill at 3414 feet by Bantry Bay in Munster, with a flat interior. In essence, most of the coastline is made up of encircling craggy uplands, and the centre of a mix of highly fertile farmland with, on the underlying impervious rock, peat bogs: some, such as the Bog of Allen, are among the world's biggest. Ireland's unique geography has created her strong national culture of language, custom and religion, since movement across and within was easier than to seaward. In consequence, the Irish have traditionally been more landsmen than seafarers. These rugged coasts have made access difficult, apart from the relatively flat expanse between Dundalk and Dublin, and this area has always been one of the most highly developed parts, where her international and English trade have flourished.

But another aspect of her geography is the moderately high but tumbled nature of the hills of Ulster to the north-east. Steep and numerous drumlins provided a natural boundary across the country and, whilst it was the last area of Ireland to be conquered by the English in the sixteenth century, it was the first to take significant immigration from Scotland in the following century. In consequence, a quite different culture developed there, which continues to be reflected by the province of Northern Ireland remaining a part of the United Kingdom.

While the fertile farmland sustained the population quite easily, over-dependence on the potato made it vulnerable to fungus leading to the massive consequent famines of 1845 and 1846. More than seven million people have left Ireland to settle overseas and America took huge numbers of Irish immigrants through Liverpool and across the Atlantic. Today there are eight times as many Irish descendants abroad as within. President Kennedy, himself of Irish ancestry, addressed the Dail Eireann, the Irish Parliament's lower house, in 1963: '…and no country contributed more to building my own than your sons and daughters'. Ireland, although a 'small' country, is thus well known – after all few other countries have produced three winners of the Nobel prize for literature.

We begin our 'tour' just south of the border between Northern Ireland and Eire. Dundalk, near Castletown river, was built around a monastic settlement by the Franciscans in about 1245, but, as the Normans had established control by then along much of eastern and southern Ireland, no castle was built there.

Abut 25 miles south along the coast at the mouth of the River Boyne, site of the battle at which William III (William of Orange) defeated the Irish, is the town of Drogheda which was founded by the Danes in 911 and was a rival to Dublin as a trading centre.

Almost exactly on the same latitude as Anglesey and Liverpool, and with a ferry connection to both of them, the capital of Eire, Dublin, was officially established in 988, when Norman Vikings settled there. There was much fighting between the Danes, the Irish and the Normans over control until the Danes were expelled in 1171 by Henry II, King of England. At the mouth of the River Liffey, Dublin was strategically placed for trade with England and the continent. It remained a small medieval town until its sacking by Oliver Cromwell in 1649, after which it grew hugely with an influx of Protestants from Europe to become the second city of the British Empire. This came at the cost of the civil rights of the Irish Catholics, who were subdued by the Anglo-Irish Protestant aristocracy. The Act of Union with Great Britain of 1801 set Dublin back until Ireland's independence from Britain in 1922 after a bloody war. Dublin is now Ireland's largest port. Exports include, of course, those from the famous Guinness Brewery, founded in 1759, although today Dublin is Ireland's leading exporter of computer hard and software manufacturing.

The original name of Wexford was Menapia, so called after a Belgic tribe who occupied the area, while the current name derives from the Viking Waesfjord – the harbour of the mud flats.

The Celts occupied Wexford over 6000 years ago. Primitive agriculture and stock rearing was the principal means of sustenance for the community. The Vikings invaded Wexford in the late eighth century. Less than two centuries later County Wexford was to be the springboard for an invasion by the Normans.

Oliver Cromwell's 1649 Irish campaign started in Wexford and included the capture of the castles at Ferns and Enniscorthy and the town. Nearby, Courtown Harbour was completely undeveloped until the Courtown family built the harbour. It soon became a thriving fishing village, and with the advent of the Dublin railway line in 1863, tourists came to enjoy the many beaches. In the age of sail and steam Wexford ships would make regular journeys to far-flung shores.

Wexford prides itself on its award winning quay front, where a statue of Commodore John Barry, the local man who founded the American Navy during the War of Independence, proudly stands on Crescent Quay. Wexford Wildfowl Reserve runs both the North and South 'slobs' of Wexford Harbour. Nearby Ballinesker Beach was the location of the Normandy landing scenes for Spielberg's epic, *Saving Private Ryan* (1998).

Kilmuckridge with its adjoining Morriscastle Beach is a popular village with excellent fishing waters. The coastline here is known as the golden mile among locals, and is now designated as a natural heritage area.

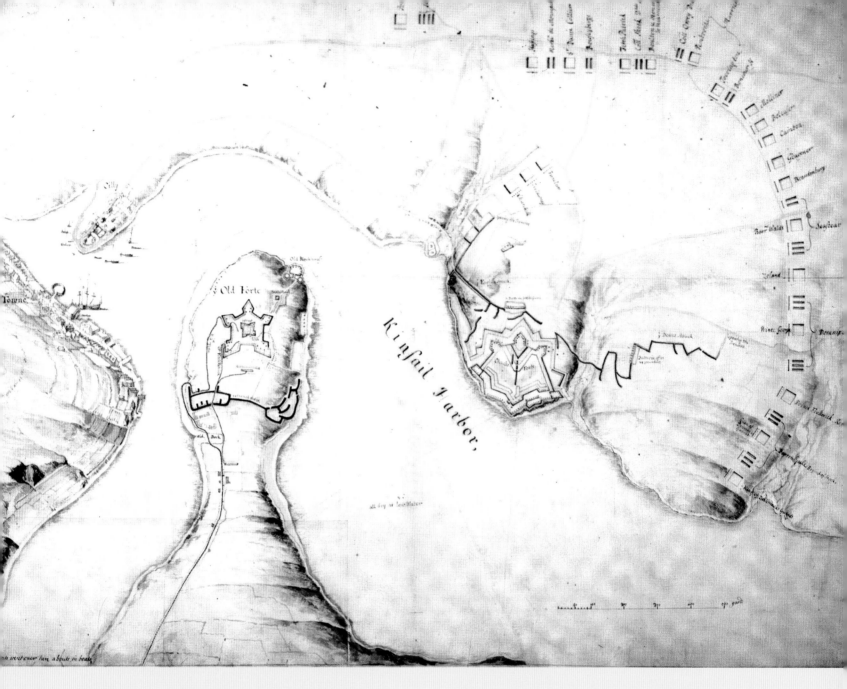

Old Forte

Kinsail Harbor

| SIEGE OF KINSALE, 1690 | The Earl of Tyrconnell, Lord Deputy of Ireland, and the Irish Catholics supported the deposed James II when he landed at Kinsale in March 1650 with a strategy of taking Ireland before crossing to invade England. William III, however, met and defeated James at the Battle of the Boyne in July, and the Duke of Marlborough then laid siege to Kinsale. This view shows the town, harbour, River Brandon, Fort Charles and the Old Fort, as well as the position of the British forces. (By permission of the British Library: ADD61343.B)

Stretching along the curve of the bay, Rosslare is often referred to as Wexford's original holiday resort. Blessed with almost 10 miles of safe, sandy beaches, Rosslare also offers fishing and watersports, while the Europort nearby serves both the British mainland and continental Europe with daily ferry services.

Tacumshane Lake and Carnsore Point are all designated areas of special ecological importance, both nationally and internationally, and are very popular with bird-watchers.

Hook Head, where the monks of Dubhán from the sixth century maintained a shipping beacon, has a lighthouse tower dating from the late twelfth or early thirteenth century, sill functioning as a beacon.

The Normans founded the town of New Ross, which is located on the estuary of the River Barrow. Both Viking and Norman influences can be discerned in the castles, abbeys, monasteries and churches of the surrounding area. The River Barrow was used to ship produce from breweries, mills and farms around the world. Through the port of New Ross, thousands of Irish people emigrated to the New World, settling in America, Australia, New Zealand and Canada.

Youghal (Eochaill, pronounced yawl) another medieval port fortified by the fifteenth-century Tynte's Castle, lies at the mouth of the River Blackwater. Its purpose was denied as the river silted up and changed course. Richard Boyle, first Earl of Cork, bought

| VIEW OF LONDONDERRY, C. 1680 | This north-east, coloured view of Londonderry is believed to be by a Thomas Phillips, one of Charles II's engineers, who worked on the defences of various British ports, including the Channel Islands. (By permission of the British Library: MAPS.K.Top.54.33.a)

the estate from Sir Walter Raleigh, who had been granted the town by Elizabeth I.

The County of Cork, tucked inside a gap in the coast that widens into a large natural harbour from where the ferries to Swansea and France run, has a distinguished, but as with most Irish cities, bruised history that reflects her struggle to independent nationhood over the centuries. Supposedly started in the sixth century by St Finbarr on the site of the present 1879 cathedral, by the twelfth century it was the chief city of the Kingdom of South Munster, but then was ruled by the English, changing hands often between the English Crown and Irish, including William III, the unforgiving champion of Protestantism. It witnessed, too, the brutality of the Black and Tans in 1920 and suffered in the Civil War subsequent to independence in 1921. The River Lee divides and effectively breaks the centre of Cork into an island. The old port for Cork is Cobh (pronounce Cove) and has strong transatlantic connections starting with the Sirius, the first steamship across the Atlantic in 1838. The Titanic made her last stop here, and the survivors of the Lusitania, sunk by a German U-boat in 1915 which contributed to America's entry into the First World War in 1917, were brought here. The world's first yacht club, the Royal Cork Yacht Club, was founded in 1720,

now based at Crosshaven, while today cruise liners stopover for arranged coach tours for their passengers. Adjacent is Spike Island and Haulbowline Island, both a British and Irish Naval Service naval base.

In September 1601 a Spanish fleet at anchor by Kinsale was attacked by the English and the Irish army that marched the length of Ireland to join them in insurrection was defeated too; in consequence all Catholics were banned for 100 years. Rightly or wrongly, it gave the impetus to develop Kinsale as a shipbuilding port and add British navy facilities until they were transferred to Haulbowline Island in Cork in 1811. Charles Fort was built 1½ miles east in the seventeenth century and, in spite of the British destruction on withdrawal in 1921, remains one of the best preserved star forts in Europe. Kinsale Harbour is now one of Ireland's premier yacht havens.

Baltimore lies at the head of the River Ilen, where the harbour is dominated by the Dún na Sead (Fort of Jewels) built as one of nine castles by the O'Driscoll clan with a white landmark beacon on the headland. It swells in the summer with sail boats, sea anglers and divers, and visitors to Cape Clear Island to the south, 5 miles long with nothing more between you and America except the notorious Fastnet Rock, the halfway mark for the famous yacht race. It is known as Ireland's teardrop, the last sight of Ireland for many emigrants, which lies a further 9½ miles south-west of Cape Clear Island. The present light is 147 feet high, the highest and widest light in the Isles of Great Britain and was built in 1897 of 2000-plus blocks of Cornish granite. Like nearly all lighthouses, it is unmanned but run by the Commissioners of Irish Lights.

The long southern coast of County Cork and Kerry, the south-western part of Ireland, is a highly indented, fjord-like shore of sea inlets, seaside resorts and ports with medieval castles and well-known beautiful peninsulas that punch out into the Atlantic, such as Mizen Head, Sheep's Head and The Beara, with such well-known off-shore islands as Scariff and the Skelligs.

To the north the land flattens as it stretches towards the River Shannon, which forms the boundary between Kerry and County Clare. The south side is mainly agricultural, while Limerick is the town that developed with a massive castle completed by King John in 1212. The quays built at the confluence of the Abbey and Shannon rivers became the commercial hub for sailing ships that travelled the 60 miles up from the river's mouth.

The coast continues north in County Clare and has dramatic limestone cliff-scapes, called the Burren, which represent the most extensive limestone region in the British Isles.

Galway is the significant port in the area, strategically placed at the mouth of the River Corrib. In 1396 Richard II granted a charter to the city transferring power to the 14 tribes (or merchant families) of Galway. For the next century Galway was trading wine, spices, fish and salt with Portugal and Spain, rivalling Bristol and London. But a fire in 1473 set the city back, and then Cromwell's armies besieged and ravaged it in 1652, followed by William III's attack, and Galway declined until modern times.

The isolated coasts and beaches of County Mayo and Sligo and their many islands belie their undiscovered beauty. The pirate, Grace O'Malley, lived on Clare Island at the mouth of Clew Bay and sailed with her crew of 200 to terrorise merchant ships into paying her a duty for safe passage to Galway port. A thousand French troops made another invasion attempt at Killala Bay in 1798 expecting the local Irish to join them in rebellion, but Lord Cornwallis, the Lord Lieutenant of Ireland, who had surrendered to the Americans in 1784, wasn't going to be beaten again.

Donegal's coastline is the longest in the country made up of precipitous cliffs and innumerable peninsulas with miles of sandy beaches. The desolate and mountainous Inishowen peninsula is formed by Lough Swilly to the west and Lough Foyle to the East reaching north to the Atlantic to stop at Ireland's most northerly point, Malin Head. It is the last remaining outpost of the Corncrake bird, that winters in Africa and whose numbers have fallen from hundreds of thousands to just 200 last year, due to modern farming practice.

Londonderry is the fifth largest city in Ireland and is at the head of Lough Foyle. It still has its town walls intact, built between 1614 and 1619. It stood out stoutly for Parliament during the English Civil War and for William III, and famously withstood the Catholic forces for 105 days until a relief ship with supplies and food burst though and broke the siege. During the nineteenth century Londonderry was one of the main emigration points for America, and reputedly supplied both sides of the US Civil War with linen shirts for their soldiers. The city still sends 12 free shirts annually to the US President.

The Giant's Causeway, a UNESCO World Heritage Site and National Nature Reserve, is famous for its regular, packed, hexagonal basalt columns. The mythology is of the Irish giant, Finn MacCool, who crossed the causeway to fight the Scottish giant Benandonner, found him asleep but much bigger than himself, so returned to Ireland. When Benandonner climbed across the Causeway, Finn's wife dressed MacCool in baby clothes and told Benandonner not to waken the child. Benandonner thought that if the baby was this size, then Finn must be huge, and fled tearing up the causeway en route, but leaving the two ends at Antrim and the Isle of Staffa in Scotland.

Belfast comes from the Irish Beál Feirste – 'mouth of the sandbank'. It wasn't really developed until 1611 by Baron Arthur Chichester, who built the castle. In the seventeenth century the first waves of Scottish and English settlers arrived, followed by Protestant Huguenots fleeing France, who laid the foundations of the Irish linen industry. Other industries, such as rope-making, tobacco, engineering and ship-building grew and the population to man these industries also expanded to overtake Dublin's by 1914 with a city of 400,000. After the partition, Belfast became the capital of Northern Ireland. Now the euphemistically named 'troubles' of the 1960s and 1970s seem to be behind them, with high employment and a buoyant housing and tourist market. Bangor is to Belfast as Brighton is to London and has its own railway connection to Belfast on which many commute from the 'Gold Coast'. Ards peninsula encloses Strangford Lough, where large colonies of seal abound and many species of sea bird and duck live off the mud flats on this finger of land and golden beaches.

Further round the coast is Carlingford, just by the border between Northern Ireland and Eire. This town is at the entrance to 'Carling ford' Lough and is noted for its historical buildings, including King John's early thirteenth-century castle, built to guard the entrance. There is another castle, Taaffe's, dating to the fifteenth century and the ruins of Carlingford Dominican Friary, founded in 1305. The town fulfils the three criteria for a port to evolve: a pre-existing settlement, usually a religious order; a commercially attractive location, again usually at the mouth of a river, and a strategic location which needed and could facilitate fortification.

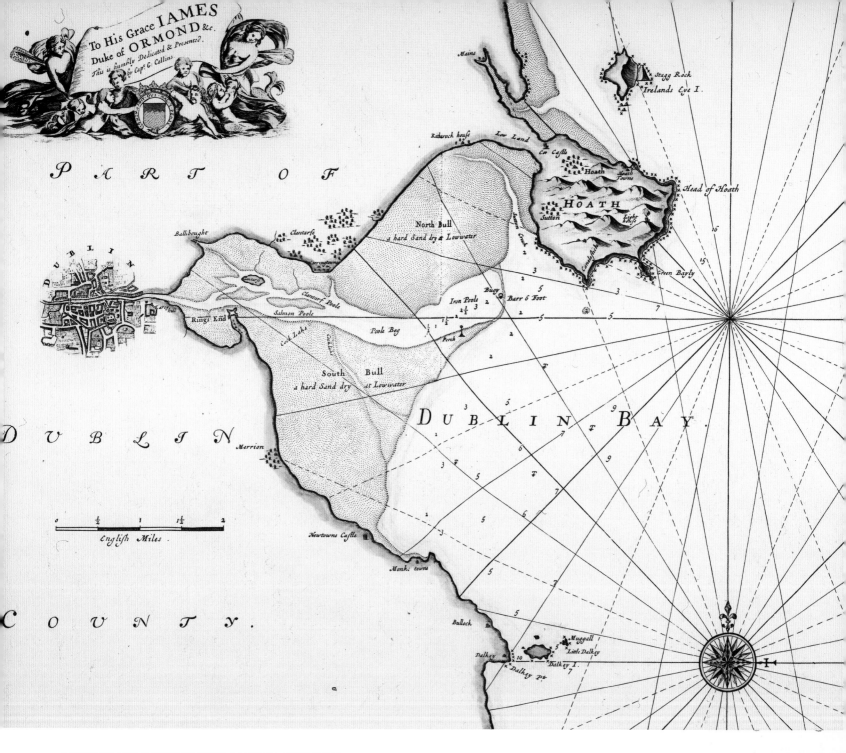

To His Grace IAMES Duke of ORMOND &c.
This is humbly Dedicated & Presented
by Capt G. Collins.

PART OF

DUBLIN

COUNTY.

DUBLIN BAY.

HOATH

North Bull
a hard Sand dry at Lowwater

South Bull
a hard Sand dry at Lowwater

Rings End

Ballibought

Clantarfe

Merrion

Newtowne Castle

Monk. towne

Bullock

Dalkey

English Miles.

| **DUBLIN AND DUBLIN BAY BY CAPTAIN GREENVILE
COLLINS, 1693** | Collins' survey, published in 1693, was relied upon
until Commander William Mudge was appointed to survey the east Irish
coasts, being by that time (1826) 'in a sadly neglected state'. Mudge
started the survey using hired boats, but after working along the coast off
County Louth in open boats he died of a chill in 1837. His Lieutenant,
George Frazer, who had ample experience from work in the English
Channel under Captain Martin White and in the St Lawrence in Canada,
took over and worked solidly for the next 15 years on this stretch of the
Irish coast in a variety of boats including the paddle steamers Comet and
Lucifer, and then in HMS Sparrow. For his formidable coastal surveying
effort and opening up the port of Dublin, Frazer was honoured by the city.
(UKHO © British Crown Copyright)

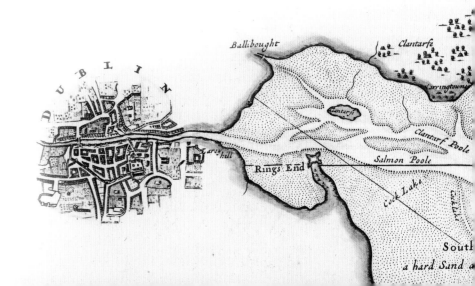

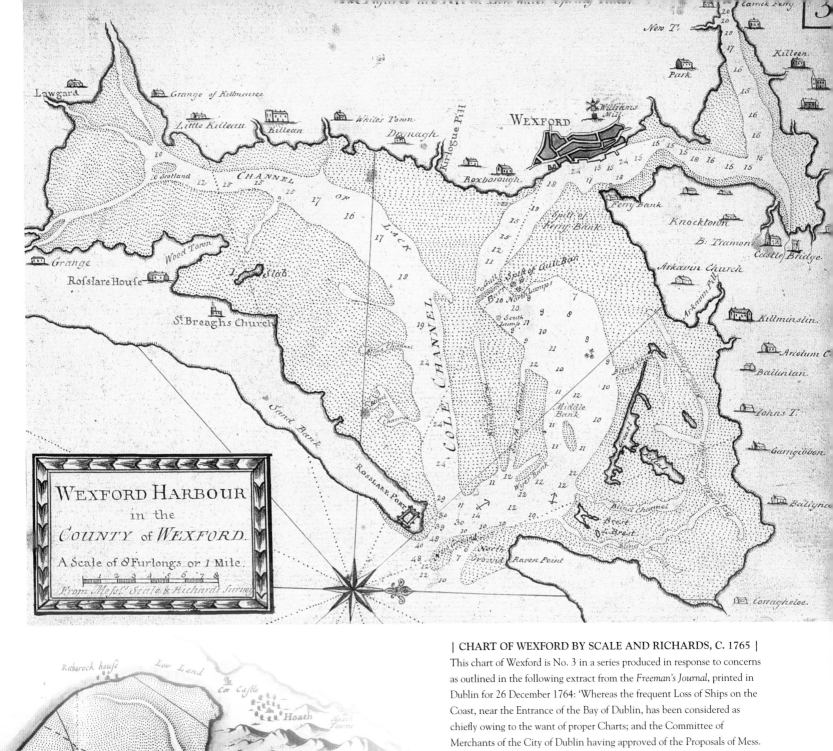

WEXFORD HARBOUR in the COUNTY of WEXFORD.

A Scale of 8 Furlongs or 1 Mile.

From Messrs. Scale & Richards Survey

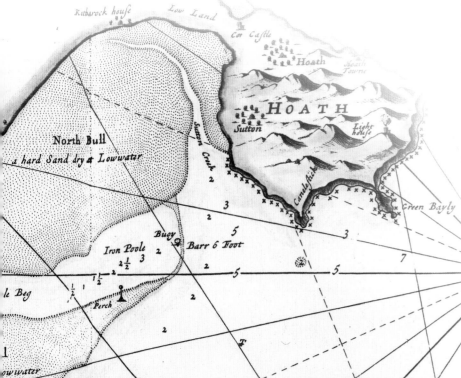

| CHART OF WEXFORD BY SCALE AND RICHARDS, C. 1765 |

This chart of Wexford is No. 3 in a series produced in response to concerns as outlined in the following extract from the *Freeman's Journal*, printed in Dublin for 26 December 1764: 'Whereas the frequent Loss of Ships on the Coast, near the Entrance of the Bay of Dublin, has been considered as chiefly owing to the want of proper Charts; and the Committee of Merchants of the City of Dublin having approved of the Proposals of Mess. Scale and Richards, for making a Survey and publishing a Chart of the Coast from Wicklow Head to Skerring, Notice is hereby given that the same will speedily be carried into Execution in the best Manner, under the Sanction and Encouragement of said Committee'.

The chart, oriented with North to the right, shows Rosslare Fort at the end of the peninsula where today, further south, the Rosslare to Fishguard ferry terminal lies, and the Gull Bar across the channel that leads to the jetty of the old town, which needs to be dredged to keep it clear. (Admiralty Library Manuscript Collection: MSS 3587)

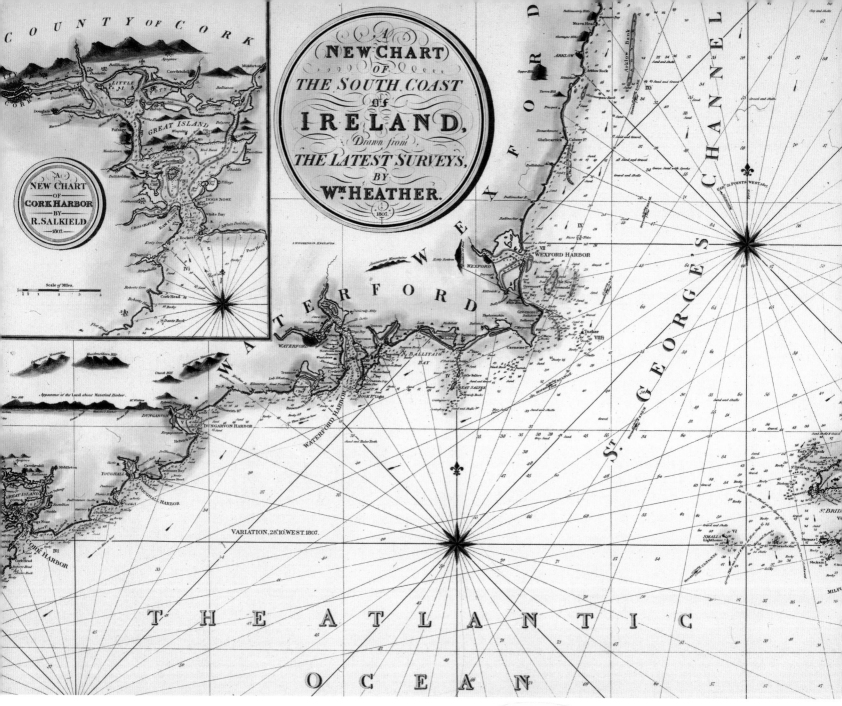

| THE SOUTH-EAST COAST OF IRELAND FROM ARKLOW TO CORK BY WILLIAM HEATHER, 1807 | Part of Heather's The Maritime Atlas or Seaman's Complete Pilot, issued between 1804 and 1808, the chart shows the south-east coast of Ireland from Mizen Head, southwards including Arklow, Wexford Harbour and Tuskar Rock, Waterford, Dungarvan to Cork, with an inset chart of Cork Harbour by R Salkield.

Heather's charts are distinctively recognisable from their elaborate and decorative script surrounded by a plain outline. He sold charts successfully for nearly 50 years from his Leadenhall Street premises, during a time in which London had become the most important centre for chart production. Charles Dickens wrote in *Dombey and Son* (published in instalments between 1846 and 1848) of the 'Navigation Warehouse' and 'Naval Academy', which were the addresses in Leadenhall Street by which Heather's business was known. (UKHO © British Crown Copyright)

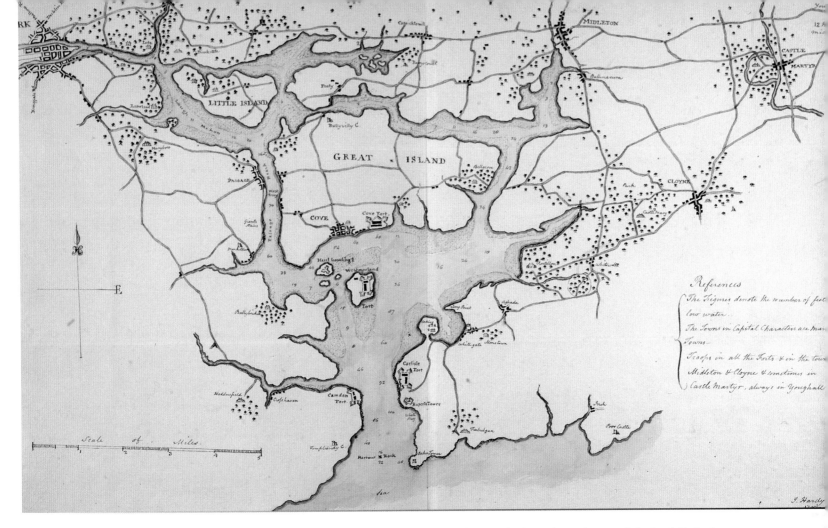

| ABOVE | CORK HARBOUR, 1797 | Cork is a natural deep-water defensible harbour. The narrow entrance channel averages 1 mile wide and the entrance is screened by Spike Island immediately to the north of the channel. The main anchorage to the east of the harbour could take a fleet of 9 battleships, 2 cruisers and 12 destroyers during the First World War. During the Napoleonic Wars its strategic importance was understood: the British fleet could quickly reach the favourable south-westerly wind to intercept any French fleet leaving the port of Brest, service a blockade there with relieving ships and cover the Channel approaches.

The Act of Union of 1801 was designed to unite Ireland with England, Scotland and Wales under Parliament in London. Thomas Pelham, 2nd Earl of Chichester, was MP for Sussex and sat in the Irish Parliament for Carrick and Armagh, and, before becoming Home Secretary in 1801, was Chief Secretary to the Lord Lieutenant of Ireland. When this map of Cork Harbour was produced by J Hardy in 1797 it was used by Pelham, and comes from the Pelham papers now held by the British Library. It gives a cogent geographical insight into Cork at this time. (By permission of the British Library: ADD.33105)

| ABOVE | VIEW OF CORK HARBOUR, C. 1660 | The west entrance of Cork Harbour with Haulbowline Island, Spike Island and Crosshaven. (By permission of the British Library: MAPS.K.Top.52.9.6)

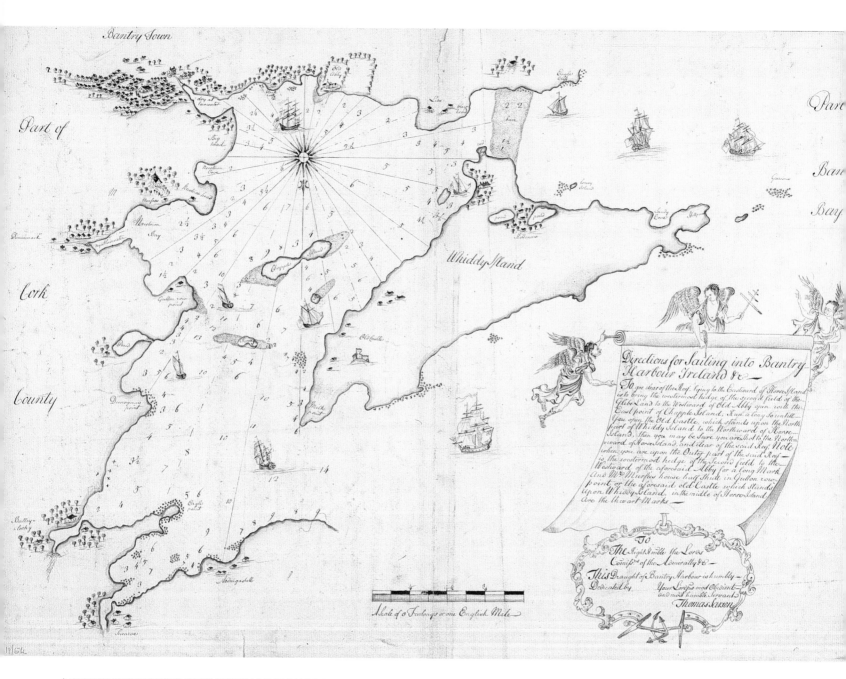

| **CHART OF BANTRY BAY BY THOMAS SARSON, LATE
EIGHTEENTH CENTURY** | Thomas Sarson was probably a master in
the Royal Navy; he dedicates this chart to the Lords Commissioners of the
Admiralty. It would have been sent to the Admiralty, as required by them,
although he might also have submitted it to one of the London chart publishers
and been paid accordingly. With a scale of 8 furlongs (in this case 250 yards) it
shows the inner part of Bantry Bay, with Whiddy Island and Bantry Harbour,
marking rocks and shoals.

The Irish name for Bantry is Beanntraige, meaning the territory of Beannt
MacNessa, son of one of the Kings of Ireland at the time of Christ. Bantry Bay is
one of the finest and safest harbours in Europe, deep watered and sheltered from
most winds by the surrounding mountains. For centuries the fleets of England,
Spain, France and Holland fished in the bay, paying harbour dues and fishing tax
to the O'Sullivan Clan who controlled it. In the last 20 years Bantry had become
a leader in mariculture with mussels the main product in a vibrant market town.
(Admiralty Library Manuscript Collection: Vz 11/54)

| ABOVE | NAVIGATIONAL VIEW OF THE ENTRANCE TO
KILLALOE, 1848 | Killaloe, in County Clare, stands at the exit of Lough
Derg, the waters from which flow through Limerick as the River Shannon.

This attractive navigational view, as part of the survey of the Lough, shows the entrance at the western end of the lake towards Killaloe and names the chief features, which are keyed on the view by flying birds. This was a device used quite often by Victorian surveyors. Important features were marked with sea birds to key the written notes instead of numbers. (UKHO © British Crown Copyright)

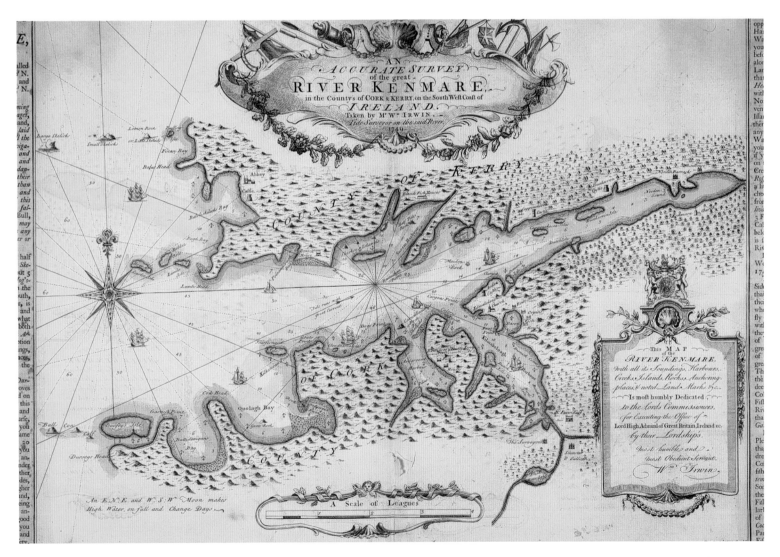

| ABOVE | SURVEY OF THE RIVER KENMARE BY WILLIAM IRWIN,
1749 | More is known about the publisher of this chart, Nathaniel Hill, than
about William Irwin, who is described as a Tide Surveyor. However, he has made a
very credible survey of the River Kenmare on the south-west coast of Ireland . Hill was an engraver and globe-maker who flourished in Chancery Lane, London, at the sign of the Globe and Sun between about 1730 and 1768. He also engraved, amongst other maps and charts, the title page and 25 charts of Lewis Morris's survey of the Welsh coast. (Admiralty Library Manuscript Collection: Vz 11/52)

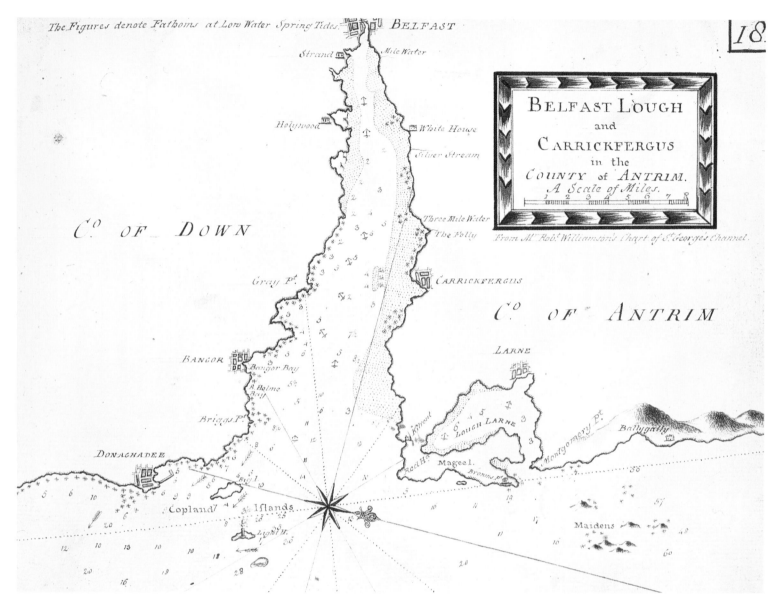

| ABOVE | CHART OF BELFAST LOUGH BY MASTER ROBERT WILLIAMSON, LATE EIGHTEENTH CENTURY | Master Williamson prepared this chart of Belfast Lough, showing the approaches to the port, with shoals, rocks and anchorages, and the main landmark buildings that were visible from the sea. (Admiralty Library Manuscript Collection: MSS 358)

| OPPOSITE | CARLINGFORD LOUGH BY CAPTAIN GREENVILE COLLINS, 1693 | Captain Collins' survey of Carlingford Lough shows the rocks with 'no passage' at the entrance, but a safe leading bearing to steer in on such that the building on the low land to the north is in line with Dundrum mountain peak, along with a profile appearance of the mountains as you approach them heading NNE by ½E, 2 leagues (6 miles) off, which is where he has drawn the leading bearing.

Local legend tells that as the giant Finn MacCool died he transformed into Carlingford Mountain, which has a body shape, and as he lay down he threw a piece of Irish earth into the sea, which became the Isle of Man.

The Lough, now a beautiful area to walk around, was used as a safe anchorage for William III's ships in 1689, but the harbour of Carlingford declined once the Newry Canal was opened in 1742. One of the four main canals in Ireland, the Newry was built to transport coal speedily from Lough Neagh and on to Dublin as English coal became too expensive to bring across the Irish Sea. (UKHO © British Crown Copyright)

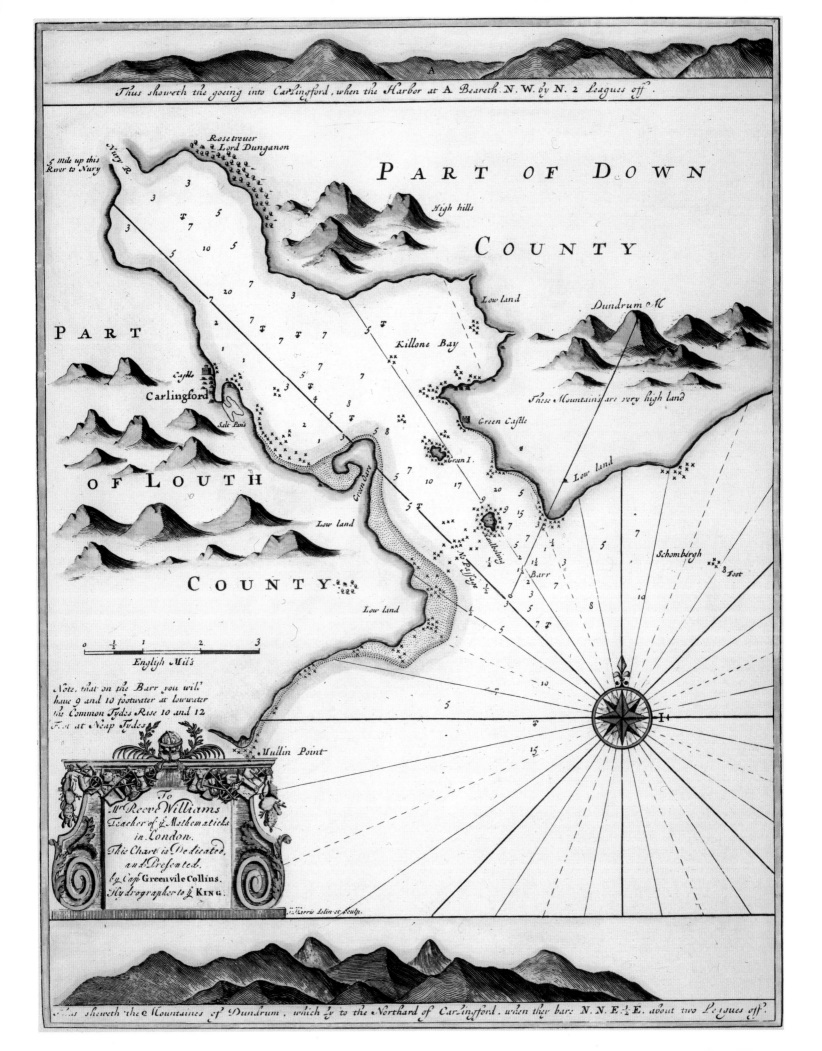

Thus showeth the goeing into Carlingford, when the Harbor at A Beareth. N.W. by N. 2 Leagues off.

PART OF DOWN

COUNTY

High hills

Rosetreuer
Lord Dunganon

Nury R.

5 mile up this
River to Nury

3

3

7

5

3

5

10

5

20

7

3

PART

7

2

7

T

7

5

1

1

Castle

Carlingford

Salt Pans

OF LOUTH

Killone Bay

Low land

Green Castle

Dundrum M.

These Mountain's are very high land

5

3

5

5

4

8

2

7

T

7

1

Green I.

Green Vary

Low land

COUNTY

5

8

5

7

10

17

20

5

Low land

9

9

15

7

7

Schomberg

x 8 foot

Santbolm

No Passage

No Passage

1
½

1
½

Barr

7

1
¼

3

5

7

1
½

½

3

5

7

T

5

7

T

8

10

7

Low land

5

10

English Mil's

0   ½   1   2   3

Note, that on the Barr you will
haue 9 and 10 footwatter at lowwater
the Common Tydes Rise 10 and 12
Feet at Neap Tydes.

Mullin Point

5

7

T

15

To
Mr Reeve Williams
Teacher of ye Mathematicks
in London.
This Chart is Dedicated,
and Presented,
by Capt Greenvile Collins.
Hydrographer to ye King.

I. Harris delin et Sculp.

Thus showeth the Mountaines of Dundrum, which ly to the Northard of Carlingford. when they bare N.N.E ½ E. about two Leagues off.

Ross kill

Shore kore very high and Steep

Castle

Half Moon

Talbooth

West Shore

Dolphin

Dolphin

Dolphin

Dolphin

West Pier

Beacon

30 foot

Lanthorn kept alwayd lighte

Port for Vessells at Low Water

Fort

Rocks Coverd by one hours flood

Noble and Righ
mmissionees of the
Brittain.
e Toun & Harbour
s Humbly Inscribd by
rovost
s Chryslie & Ro! Angus
Burgh. 1745.

I. E. delin.

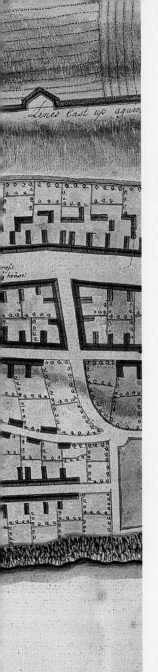

CHAPTER VI

SCOTLAND

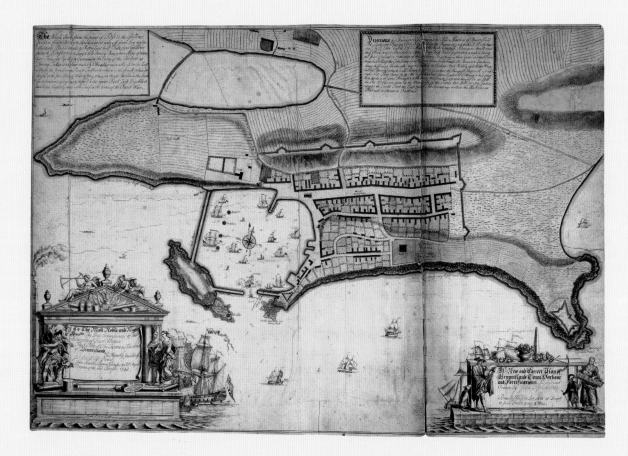

| PLAN OF BURNTISLAND TOWN, HARBOUR AND FORTIFICATIONS BY JOHN ELPHINSTONE, 1745 | Elphinstone's plan shows the salient features to plan the defences, perhaps with a view to the overall use of the harbour, during the Jacobite rebellion. Interesting details include his advice where ships up to 200 tons could careen and at the entrance: the 'Lanthorn, keep it always lighted'. The ship leaving harbour would appear to be giving a gun salute.

Burntisland was a significant naval port, and shipbuilding an important industry. The harbour was involved in naval activity over the centuries. The French tried to land there in 1560, and troops stood to in preparation to fight off the Spanish Armada in 1588. The ferry *The Blessing of Burntisland* was anything but for Charles I when she sank with his treasure crossing the Firth of Forth, and Cromwell's ships bombarded the town and took it, unpopularly garrisoning it for nine years. The Dutch responded to privateers operating out of the harbour by bombarding it in 1667. (Admiralty Library Manuscript Collection: Vz 11/53)

THE geographical border between England and Scotland may have been defined through centuries of armed conflict but the fishing border in the Solway Firth is still ambivalent as England and Scotland have their own fishing laws. National borders have often been a source of contention in the past and maps and charts have tried to define them – but economic prerogatives often override, and so the Cumbrian ports of England took the shipping trade from the Scottish ports of Kirkcudbright, Annan and the River Nith, unable to cope with bigger ships. This coast of Dumfries and Galloway is as varied as any in the British Isles with shingle beaches at Burrow Head, impressive headlands at Abbey Head and the peninsula at the Mull of Galloway and long sandy beaches in Luce Bay. The nearest point of Scotland to Ireland is Portpatrick, about 22 miles, but the harbour was ruined by storms at the end of the nineteenth century and now caters for tourists.

The coast turns north-east past Loch Ryan, which gives a sheltered approach to the Clyde for Scotland-to-Ireland ferries to and from Stranraer and Larne. The coast mainly comprises sand dunes held down by sea-grass which have provided links for well-known golf courses such as Turnberry. The large granite boss of Ailsa Craig is very visible from this coast, shaped by glaciers, with rock boulders from here found in the south of England. Glaswegian prosperity required leisure and the sea towns of this coast such as Ayr and Largs grew accordingly. Across the Firth of Clyde the Isle of Arran used to host the Royal Navy Dreadnought battleships in the deep-water anchorage at Lamlash.

The Firth of Clyde from the west coast and the Firth of Forth from the east coast cut into the land to such an extent that it is understandable that the early cartographers thought Scotland was an island separate from England. As Daniel Defoe discovered on his map during his 1720s tour: 'when I came more critically to examine the ground, I found the map-makers greatly mistaken, and that they had not only given the situation and courses of the rivers wrong, but the distances also'.

Glasgow, however, was not a natural port and Irvine, some 50 miles away on the approach to the Firth of Clyde, was used until dredging allowed Glasgow to develop in the eighteenth century importing sugar, rum and tobacco (the tobacco profits paid for the large mansions in the town), and in the nineteenth century, to become a cotton importer and exporter of iron and steel products. Its shipbuilding and railway locomotive industry developed along the River Clyde in the late nineteenth century so that by the Edwardian period almost one third of the world's shipping was built there. It is hard to believe that it started as a little salmon-fishing village at a River Clyde crossing. Little is left of the shipbuilding now but Glasgow has transformed itself into a town of self-pride and full employment in the service industries. The other destination in which to relax is across the Firth of Clyde by ferry from Wemyss Bay to Rothesay on the Isle of Bute.

The western coasts along the Highlands of Scotland have their own character formed by glacier-scored peninsulas, headlands and sea lochs such as Loch Fyne and Loch Linnhe, which intrude some 50 miles into the land, the latter to Fort William. There are many islands off shore, which form the island groups of the Inner and Outer Hebrides.

This coast has few good natural harbours until you get as far north as Ullapool, the largest fishing port on the west coast. Oban has a fine harbour, is connected by rail to Glasgow, is popular as a resort, and has a ferry connection through the Sound of Mull to the islands of South Uist and Barra in the Outer Hebrides, and to Colonsay south along the Firth of Lorn.

The Hebrides are a group of over 50 islands to the west and north-west of Scotland, although only one fifth of them are inhabited. The Outer Hebrides or Western Isles (also known as Long Island) are made up of the Isles of Lewis and Harris, Taransay, North Uist, Benbecula, South Uist, Barra and St Kilda. They are separated from the Inner Hebrides by straits, the Minch, Little Minch and Hebrides sea. The Inner Hebrides includes the Isles of Skye, Raasey, Rum, Eigg, Coll, Tiree, Staffa, Iona, Mull, Scarba, Colonsay, Oronsay, Jura and Islay, and all enjoy a mild climate in beautiful scenery.

Part of the railway from Glasgow goes round Scotland's highest mountain, Ben Nevis at 4406 feet, to Fort William at the head of Loch Linnhe and on to Mallaig, still a fishing port. The Highland Railway from Edinburgh swings across the north-west Highlands to the Kyle of Lochalsh from where you can drive to Skye across the bridge that fords the half-mile strait of Kyle Akin.

Cape Wrath is the north-westernmost tip of Scotland, named with respect for the terror of the seas around this exposed promontory during endless storms. The population along this most northern mainland coast is centred on Dounreay, controversially known for its nuclear power station and Thurso, set in a sandy bay curving round to Dunnet Head, and from nearby Scrabster ferries run to the Orkneys.

The Orkney Islands comprise some 70 islands to the north of Scotland, of which about 20 are inhabited. The Mainland, Pomona, is the biggest, with a large anchorage almost encircled by land, Scapa Flow, which was used by the British Grand Fleet (1914–18) and Home Fleet (1939–45) during the two world wars. It is also where the German fleet was interned and scuttled at the

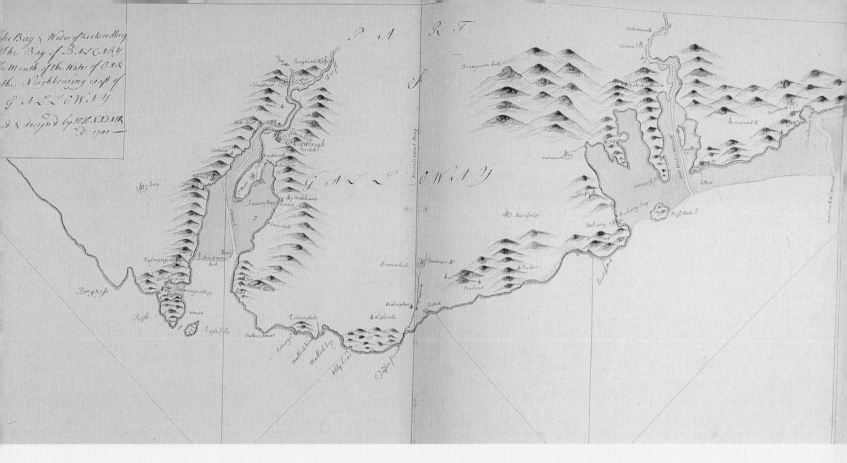

| SURVEY OF GALLOWAY AND KIRKCUDBRIGHT BY JOHN ADAIR, 1701 |

Adair's manuscript chart of Galloway and Kirkcudbright is one of the surveys he prepared in 1701, similar to the Hebridean Islands on page 104, for his Description of the Sea Coasts and Islands of Scotland, Part I, published in 1703. (Admiralty Library Manuscript Collection: MSS 331)

end of the First World War. Kirkwall and Stromness are the two towns, and other larger islands include Hoy, South Ronaldsay, Stronsay, Sanday, Westray, Rousay, Shapinsay and Eday. A windy and wet, but mild climate makes for a flat hinterland, and trees are scarce, but the farmland is rich and beef cattle, pigs and sheep are reared. In addition, the North Sea oil industry has brought much employment. Because of their Norwegian heritage, the islanders spoke their own language, 'Norn', until the eighteenth century and they have many prehistoric relics, including standing stone circles.

Some 30 miles to the north of the Orkneys lie the Shetland Isles, with about 100 islands, although fewer than 20 are inhabited. The main island is called Mainland and its port is Lerwick; the other large islands are Yell, Unst, Fetlar, Whalsey and Bressay. These are generally low and rocky, but cliffs do rise to 1000 feet. The islands were attached to Scotland in 1472 as an unredeemed pledge of Christian I of Norway and Denmark as the dowry of his daughter Margaret, who married James III of Scotland. Today, besides the famous Shetland pony, fishing, cattle and sheep rearing are important and the oil terminal built at Sullom Voe on Mainland provides significant employment, as does tourism.

One of the most difficult stretches of sea to sail through is the Pentland Firth. The scenery is spectacular with stolid geological marvels in rust-red limestone stacks and cliffs; examples are the climbers' favourite, the Old Man of Hoy, and Mendelssohn's musical inspiration, Fingal's Cave. They stand at odds with the quicksilver surge of the sea that crashes around their base, and where the sea swirls through at high speed so that even a powerful warship has to keep full power to maintain her course through the narrowing 7-mile gap between Duncansby Head (with Scotland's northernmost mainland town – John O'Groats) and the southernmost Orkney Island of South Ronaldsay. Not all ships have been able to do this. Most take passage between the two smaller southern Orkneys of Swona and Stroma. For about half of each month on average the wind never drops below Force 7. To guide the 6000 odd shipping passages a year who take this shorter route – mainly Orkney ferries, commercial freighters and fishing trawlers – the Admiralty List of Lights names five lighthouses (they should be called light-towers to reflect the strength with which their hand-cut dove-tail jointed granite blocks are pieced together to withstand the incessant Atlantic gales): Dunnet Head, Duncansby Head, the Pentland Skerries island (3 miles south of Brough Ness on South Ronaldsay), Stroma and Swona. They form a sort of pentangle of illuminating guidance for ships transiting through the Firth. This was the scene that one ship came on as she tried to make Denmark with a full cargo. The SS Pennsylvania, of 6000 tons, hit Stroma in thick fog in 1931, and the rocks held her tight as the notorious 10-knot tide broke her keel and made her unsalvageable. Between 1918 and 1933 94 ships ran aground or hit the rocks, of which 32 sank or were total losses.

**| NAVIGATIONAL VIEW OF FAIR ISLE BY HORATIO N HESS, 1821
|** This attractive watercolour of Fair Isle was painted 3½ miles off the island looking 'NNE ½ by E' towards the forbidding cliffs. Fair Isle, known for the sweater designs that were influenced by Arab trading in medieval times, is positioned almost half way between the Orkneys and the Shetlands about 30 miles north-east of Ronaldsay. (UKHO © British Crown Copyright)

The east coast of Scotland is less striated, with fewer breathtaking cliff lines. It is smoother than the west coast, but has more opportunities for bird-life to breed on the flatter shores. There are exceptions, and immediately south of Duncansby Head are the Stacks of Duncansby, while Sinclairs Bay has a smooth strip of sandy beach for 4 miles ending by the Noss Head lighthouse, with nearby castles, Castle Girnigo and Castle Sinclair. A little further south, Wick was developed as a harbour by Thomas Telford to provide a base for up to 700 fishing boats until they moved to the larger ports along the coast. Today the herring fish shoals are out in the Atlantic; North Sea pollution has reduced their food from what was a nutrient-rich water with high plankton production, and the warming waters have driven them out to find more comfortable temperatures, so fishing boats are few.

Helmsdale is another small fishing village at the head of Strath Kildonan with coal and a little gold found in 1868. It has a waning harbour, with a distillery and woollen mill.

Dornoch, well-known for its Royal Dornoch golf links, is also appealing for its sandy beaches along the Dornoch Sands and its cathedral. The peninsula of Tarbat Ness fingers out into the North Sea to catch the unwary mariner in fog, and round the coast from it is the natural bay and anchorage of Invergordon leading into Cromarty Firth. A harbour was built in 1828 and it became an important naval base and dockyard in the twentieth century, strategically positioned to cover the approaches to the 'gateways' into the North Atlantic that, in time of conflict, the Germans would use for their U-boats, fleets or surface raiders. These gateways include the 300-mile 'gap' between the Norwegian coast and Britain, the 500-mile 'gap' between Iceland and Britain and the Denmark strait, and the 200-mile 'gap' between Iceland and Greenland. The base was closed in 1956. In 1931, during the Depression, pay cuts of 10 per cent were ineptly announced by the Board of Admiralty to the fleet on ships' notice boards. The Army and Air Force had no such cuts and the result was discontent resulting in a mass refusal to weigh anchor when the fleet was ordered to sea. The Invergordon Mutiny, as it was called, only subsided when the Admiralty retracted.

The boom in North Sea oil and gas boosted the local economy with the oil-rig building industry in the 1970s. The Moray Firth leads to Inverness at the head of the Caledonian Canal which joins with Loch Ness and Loch Lochy to continue to Fort William on the western side, giving a water transit of 55 miles. The resorts of Fortrose, with two ruined cathedrals, and Rosemarki, with its red sandstone cliffs, are divided by the headland of Chanonry Point from the well-preserved Fort George, built as the northernmost of a chain of forts designed to split and control the Highlanders.

Inverness, on the southern shores of the Firth, holds the key to this area in military terms. Oliver Cromwell fortified and garrisoned it, and it reflects the Englishness imposed on it. But the first sea port on the Moray Firth coast is Nairn, the medieval capital and a resort with good, sandy beaches. At Findhorn, a mild climate allows nearly 50 plant species to grow here, well north of their normal habitat boundary.

This coast on the south of the Moray Firth, in the county of Grampian, has a number of rocky headlands with inlets to sustain fishing ports. Buckie, Findochty and Portnockie, with a striking limestone free-standing arch, the Bow Fiddle Rock, are examples. Lossiemouth also has the old Fleet Air Arm training air station, since handed over to the RAF, while the fishing ports of Cullen and Portsoy are now tourist resorts. As found in similar rock in Cornwall, red and green serpentine used to be quarried and shipped to France. Banff, at the mouth of the River Deveron, was an important medieval trading port, beloved of the Scottish gentry in the eighteenth century with Macduff across the estuary. As Banff silted up other ports prospered. The headlands along this part reach 400 feet and are home to fulmars, kittiwakes, skuas and puffins.

At Kinnairds Head the coast curves southwards past Rattray Head and the small fishing port of old Faithlie was developed by Alexander Fraser of Philorth in 1546 into a harbour for ships passing this significant headland, Fraserburgh. After the destructive gales of the winter of 1782, when both naval and merchant fleets suffered, forceful petitions to Parliament finally resulted in a bill to build four lighthouses along the most used and dangerous parts of the Scottish coast: at the Mull of Kintyre overlooking the Firth of Clyde; at Eilean Glas by the coast of Harris; on North Ronaldsay, the northerly island of the Orkneys; and the first to be completed in 1786 by the newly appointed Northern Lighthouse Trust (now the Northern Lighthouse Board) was at Kinnairds Head by their engineer, Thomas Smith, utilising an old fortified tower. His stepson went into partnership with him and started a dynasty of four generations, including Robert Stephenson, that built the majority of Scotland's lighthouses.

Peterhead is the chief port on the Buchan coast, north of Aberdeen. It developed from a small village to become the leading British whaling port during the early 1800s until the trade transferred to Norway.

Aberdeen grew at the confluence of two of Scotland's great rivers, originally based on the Norman cathedral of St Machar at the mouth of the Don as a fishing port, and the New Town at the mouth of the Dee, expanded as a seaport and latterly as a commercial centre for the North Sea oil and gas industry.

Twenty miles further south along the huge cliffs relieved only by access to the sea at Muchalls, is the harbour of Stonehaven formed of two eighteenth-century conceived settlements, and bigger vessels gained access to the harbour when Robert Stephenson removed the pile of rocks in the entrance.

Montrose developed at the mouth of the southern River Esk, and transformed from a smugglers' haven to a resort for the eighteenth-century leisured classes.

The influence of the monks and the thirteenth-century abbey helped Arbroath to grow. The Abbot not only improved the harbour in the fifteenth century, but, as reported by Robert Stephenson, tradition has it that the Abbot of Aberbrothock (old spelling of Arbroath) 'directed a bell to be erected on the rock, so connected with a floating apparatus, that the winds and sea acted upon it and tolled the bell, thus giving warning to the mariner of his approaching danger'.

This rock is the infamous Bell or Inchcape Rock, a 700-yard-long sandstone reef lying in the North Sea about 11 miles south-east of Arbroath and 20 miles east of Dundee, but near to the fairway for ships making to and from the Firths of Tay and the Forth. As it is covered by just 16 feet of water at high tide, and exposed by a few feet at low tide, it poses a considerable danger to shipping. The erection of a lighthouse became paramount after the great gale of 1799 when 70 vessels were shipwrecked on it, including the York, a 74-gun Royal Navy ship of the line. Built by Stephenson, construction of the lighthouse could only take place at low tide and between storms, and the light first shone out in 1811.

The coast between Arbroath and Dundee makes for good golf courses and Canoustie players can see those of St Andrews across the Firth of Tay, crossed by road and rail bridges. Dundee became the premier whaling port, and lit its streets with Sperm Oil for good measure. Along the coast of the Fife peninsula are many fishing ports that caught the herring in their heyday, such as Anstruther and Pittenweem, along with iron and coal ports such as Kirkcaldy.

The Forth railway bridge, a cantilever marvel of its 1890 construction, doesn't give enough height above water for the taller ships such as an aircraft-carriers to pass beneath, and the road bridge, which opened in 1964, made Queensferry and Inverkeithing ferries redundant. The oysters caught along the coast at Musselburgh and Prestonpans used to supply Edinburgh, but pollution has depleted stocks. The land turns southwards again at North Berwick, with Bass Rock off the headland. The coast runs on with attractive cliff scenery past St Ann's Head to the border between Scotland and England a few miles north of Berwick-on-Tweed.

THE
RIVER of CLYDE
Surveyed by
JOHN WATT

N.B. The Soundings are in Fathoms
except those on Dumbuc Ford
which are in Feet at High Water
Latitude of Glasgow 55°.56 North
Long: 4° 9' West from London

REFERENCE

A Bishops Palace
B Butcher Market
C Veal Market
D Green Markets
E Slaughter house
F Dean Side
G New Vennal
H Stock Friars Wynd
K Grammar School Wynd
L Spout Mouth
M Rattan Row
N Dry Gate
O Princess Street
P Buns Wynd
R Goose Dubs
S Exchange
T Tolbooth
U New Church
W Virginia Street
X Millar Street
Y Queen Street

A Scale of English Miles.

| SURVEY OF THE RIVER CLYDE BY JOHN WATT, 1776 | The River Clyde has been the arterial trade route into and out of Scotland for centuries. With the availability of coal, iron and manpower nearby, shipbuilding was bound to develop too. The dangerous and shifting sandbanks that run between Greenock and Glasgow always need careful navigation and John Watt, uncle to James Watt, well known for his invention of the steam engine, published this chart privately in 1776, although it was quickly superseded by Professor Murdoch Mackenzie's 1776 survey.

The chart shows soundings and anchorages, the important sandbanks and the main docks and ports that served Glasgow, including Port Glasgow and Greenock, although Irvine some 50 miles from Glasgow would take the larger ships.

There are now three lighthouses on the small, 773-acre, 400-foot high island of Little Cumray (Cumbrae today), strategically placed to guide shipping northwards towards Glasgow. The second built in 1793 by Thomas Smith and his son-in-law Robert Stephenson, of the family that erected most of Scotland's lighthouses (most of which are still in use today), replaced that built in 1753, shown on this chart. The third and current automatic light was completed in 1997.

The coat of arms of Glasgow stamps the inset town plan, and much of the Gaelic word spelling gives credence to its common use at that time.
(UKHO © British Crown Copyright)

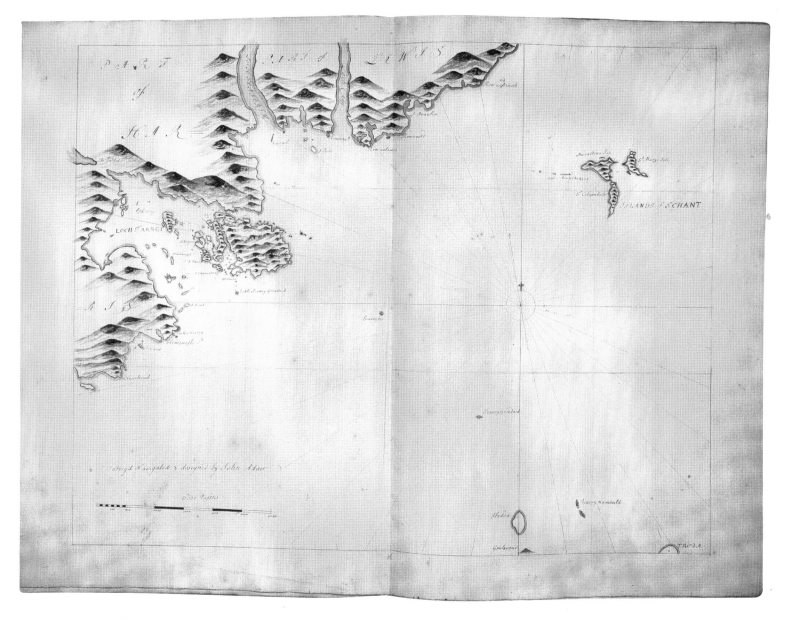

| ABOVE | MANUSCRIPT CHART OF PART OF
LEWIS AND HARRIS, LOCH TARBET, GLASS ISLAND
AND THE ISLANDS OF SCHIANT BY JOHN ADAIR,
1701 | John Adair was, like Professor Murdoch Mackenzie,
a mathematician and hydrographer. He is best known for his
Description of the Sea Coasts and Islands of Scotland, Part I,
published in 1703, and was made a Fellow of the Royal Society
two years later. But he was unable to complete Part II due to lack
of funds. This survey would seem to be one of his preparatory
charts held by the Admiralty Library in Portsmouth; others
are held in King's Library, part of the British Library, and the
Advocate's Library in Edinburgh. He received some payment for
his work – although not enough to keep him out of debt – by
two Acts of Tonnage, passed by the Privy Council of Scotland in
1695 and 1705, whereby a share was paid to him of the harbour
dues from vessels using certain Scottish ports. (Admiralty Library
Manuscript Collection: MSS 331)

| OPPOSITE BELOW | THE PENTLAND FIRTH BY
MASTER GEORGE THOMAS, 1830 | Master Thomas
commanded HM brig Investigator for 26 years until 1836,
succeeding Graeme Spence on the home water surveys, which
included Liverpool Harbour, Fowey Harbour, the Firth of Forth,
The Gatway (Yarmouth) from Orfordness to Lowestoft, the
Shetland Islands and several Orkney Islands. This survey was not
just a tricky one to carry out, but dangerous too, because of the
strength of the tidal currents through the Pentland Firth. It gives
the position of the Skerries Lighthouse and shows how the tidal
currents eddy at full flood, turning back on themselves in the
lee of the islands such as Stroma and Swona. Thomas went
on to command the Mastiff with further surveys around the
Orkneys, until he died 'in harness' in 1846, after 30 years of
almost continual surveying at sea. One tribute writes that his
surveys 'had ever the impress of accuracy and care'. (Admiralty
Library Manuscript Collection: Vy 12/29)

| OPPOSITE ABOVE |
DUNCANSBY HEAD BY
W RAMAGE, 1824 | This
navigational view of Duncansby
Head with an unusually calm
Pentland Firth off the furthest
north part of the British mainland,
is by one of the Royal Navy
hydrographers, W Ramage. From
this artwork the view to be
included on the Admiralty Chart
was prepared. (UKHO © British
Crown Copyright)

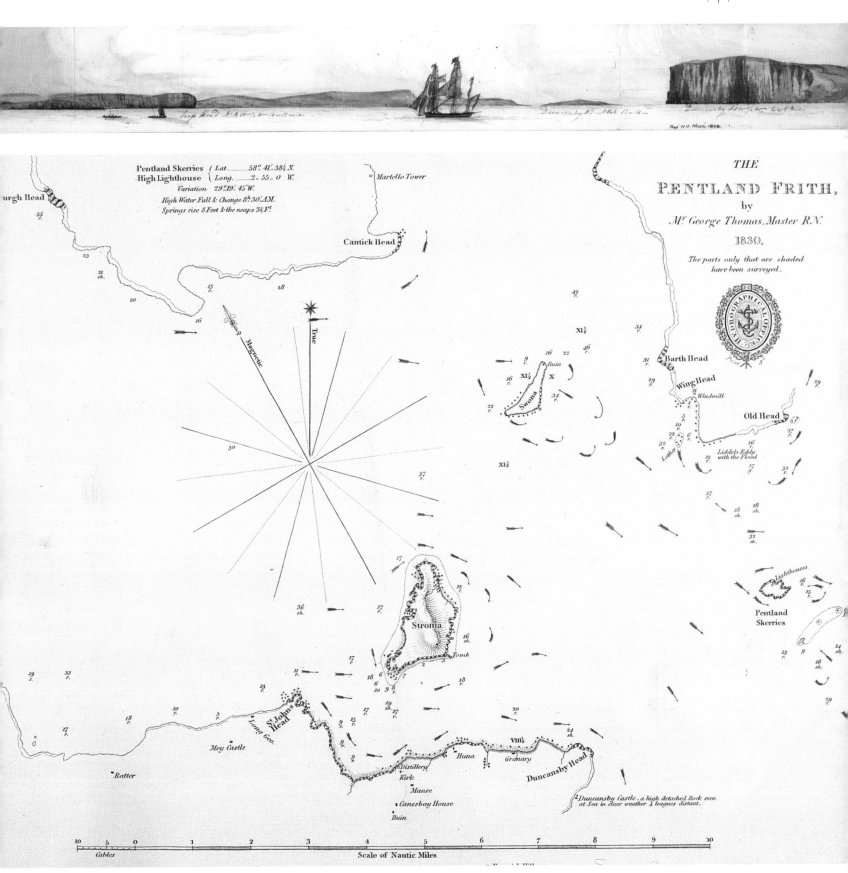

THE
PENTLAND FRITH,
by
M.r George Thomas, Master R.N.
1830.

The parts only that are shaded have been surveyed.

Pentland Skerries { Lat......58°.41'.38½' N.
High Lighthouse { Long......2..55..0 W.
Variation 29°.19'.45 W.
High Water Fall & Change 8.h 30.m A.M.
Springs rise 8 Feet & the neaps 3½ F.t

Cantick Head

Martello Tower

urgh Head

Barth Head
Wing Head
Windmill
Old Head
Liddels Eddy
with the Flood
Lothar

Swona
Ruin
X

Stroma
Tomb

Pentland
Skerries
Lighthouses

St John's Head
Long Geo
Mey Castle
Ratter
Distillery
Kirk
Manse
Canesbay House
Ruin
Huna
Granary
Duncansby Head

Duncansby Castle, a high detached Rock: seen at Sea in clear weather ¼ leagues distant.

Magnetic
True

Cables
Scale of Nautic Miles

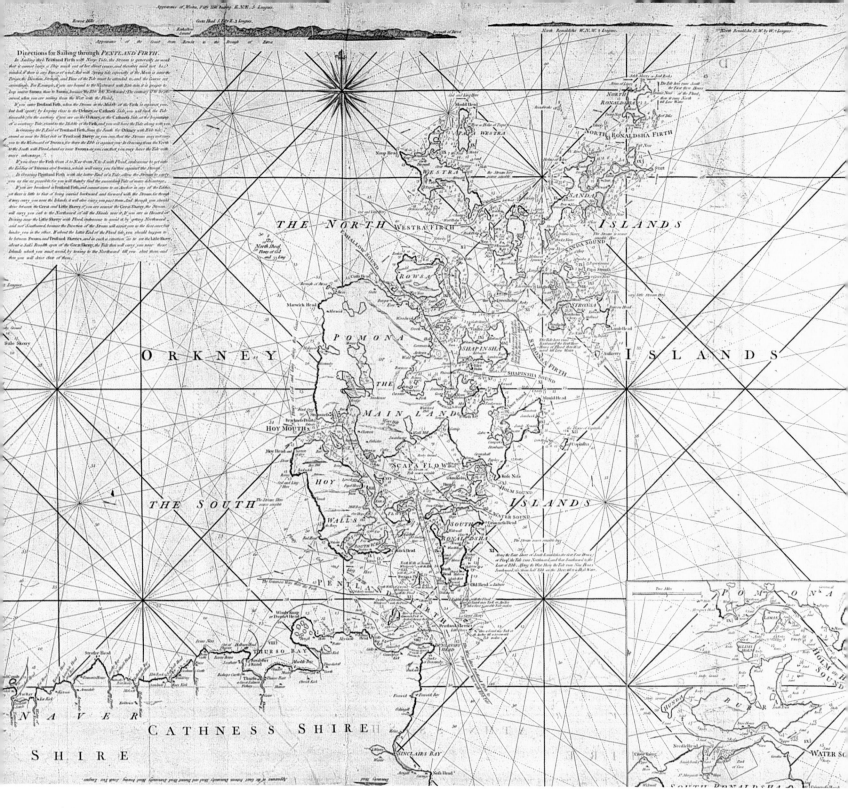

| CHART OF CAITHNESSHIRE AND THE ORKNEYS, PUBLISHED BY LAURIE AND WHITTLE IN 1794 | Covering the coast from Cape Wrath, at the north-westernmost tip, to Duncansby Head, the north-easternmost tip of Scotland, and the Orkneys, this chart was designed for the Merchant Navy captain, and has the pilot information and sailing directions included on the chart. This was to change with the advent of the Admiralty chart when a special Pilot for each area of the world would be issued to be read in conjunction with the chart. It gives suggested navigational routes through the notorious Pentland Firth and the Orkney Islands.

Robert Laurie and James Whittle published this chart, selling it in their shop in Fleet Street, London. Laurie was an accomplished mezzotinter, while Whittle

provided the PR. Although their output was prolific, they needed a continual supply of fresh information, which they received from naval officers and masters in the Royal Navy and East India Company, such as Master Francis Owen's manuscript chart of Portsmouth and Spithead and Master William Price's of the south coast of England in the 1790s.

Laurie's son, Richard Holmes Laurie, took on the business from 1818, which finally amalgamated, in the face of the overwhelming market position of the Admiralty chart as it developed during Queen Victoria's reign, into the firm we know today of Imray, Laurie, Norie and Wilson, whose chart market concentrates on the yacht and leisure sailor and fisherman. (Admiralty Library Manuscript Collection: Vu 8/20)

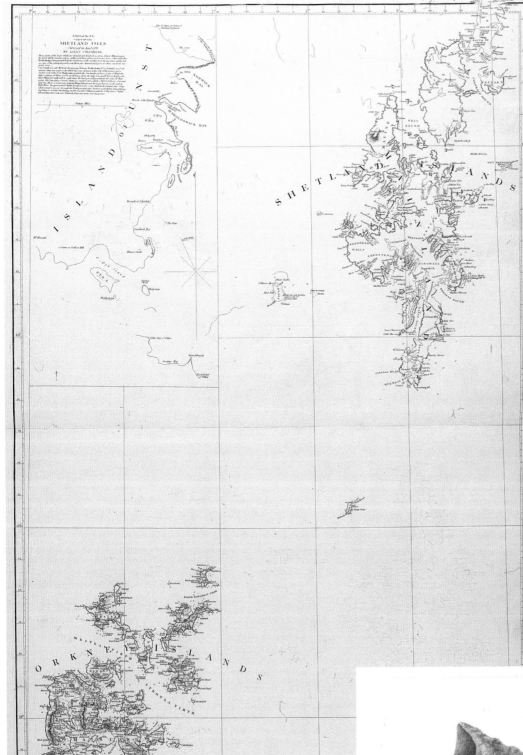

| LEFT | SHETLAND ISLANDS, ORKNEY ISLANDS AND FAIR ISLE BY LIEUTENANT EDWARD COLUMBINE, 1795 | Lieutenant Columbine was an experienced hydrographer having made surveys in the West Indies, including Trinidad, and St John's, Newfoundland. He was one of three men who made up the Admiralty Chart Committee whose purpose was to review urgently the existing commerical charts, check them for accuracy and organise their distribution, the other two being Captain Sir Home Popham, and Captain Thomas Hurd. The Committee was set up on 27 November 1807 over concern that the ageing Hydrographer, Alexander Dalrymple, was not actually getting charts out to the fleet quickly enough. A year later Hurd replaced Dalrymple as Hydrographer when Their Lordships deemed it 'expedient to remove you'.

The chart shows most of the islands' coasts but those in outline are not surveyed. (Admiralty Library Manuscript Collection: Vy 12/20)

| BELOW | VIEW OF HANG CLIFF, SHETLAND, BY C PALMER, 1818 | This dramatic view was taken from HMS Dorothea, commanded by Captain David Buchan, as she made her way in company with the brig Trent, commanded by Lieutenant (later Admiral Sir) John Franklin on an expedition to penetrate the sea as far north as possible and survey parts of the North American coastline. Captain Buchan would have instructed Palmer to paint this view as they made their way north-east towards Spitzbergen. (UKHO © British Crown Copyright)

HANG CLIFF Shetland bearing South 6 Miles
taken from HMS Dorothea David Buchan Esq.r Captain 10 May 1818

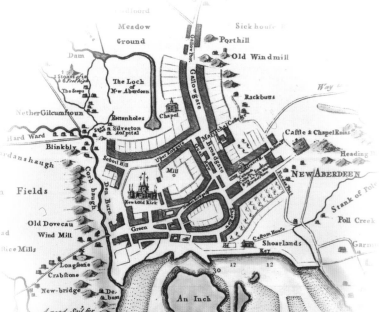

| CHART OF ABERDEEN BY G & W PATERSON, 1746 | This survey of Old and New Aberdeen shows, with a wealth of interesting detail on the land and advice as to the best vegetables ('a good Soil for Turnips, Parsnips, Carrots and all sort of Potherbs which y inhabitants daily use'), how the two towns were still separated by meadows and fields, and their situation between the two river outlets into what was then called the German Sea.

The town started to make its money through granite quarrying which only stopped in 1971. Other early industries included papermaking from 1694, woollens in 1703, linen in 1749 and cotton in 1779. A wooden shipbuilding industry thrived and the Aberdeen tea clippers were respected winners of the tea races from Canton. The deep-sea fishing industry grew to rival Grimsby's and daily fish trains ran to London. Jam, pickle and potted meats became important, with many acres of strawberries and other fruits growing in the adjacent countryside. Aberdeen responded to the discovery of North Sea oil and gas in the late twentieth century and became the centre of Europe's petroleum industry, servicing the off-shore oil rigs. (UKHO © British Crown Copyright)

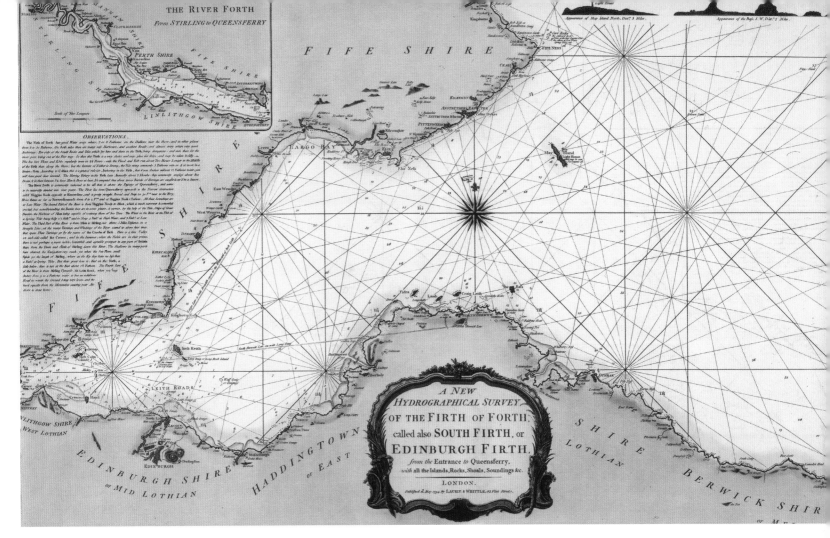

| ABOVE | FIRTH OF FORTH PUBLISHED BY LAURIE AND
WHITTLE IN 1794 | Laurie and Whittle published this survey of the
Firth of Firth on 12 May 1794. The Merchant Navy liked this clear style of
chart presentation and the scale, which suited their manner of navigation.
With sailing directions and an inset chart of the River Forth towards Stirling,
views of Bass Rock and May Island, the chart combines a 'grid' of a circular
set of compass roses (although only five are drawn) based on a central rose
and gives latitude and longitude.

A number of ports and harbours grew up around the Firth, at Leith, which
is Edinburgh's port, at Kirkcaldy and Musselburgh, out of which fishing boats
operate, and the navy had a dockyard at Rosyth for many years. (UKHO ©
British Crown Copyright)

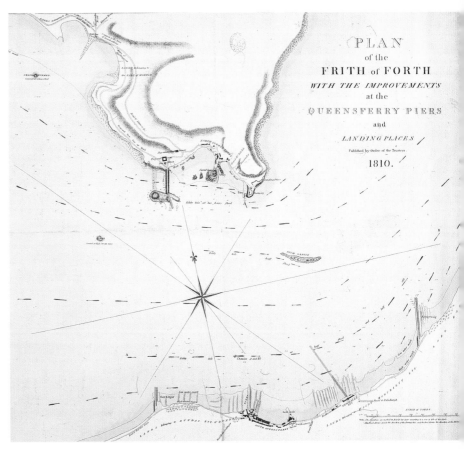

| RIGHT | PLAN OF QUEENSFERRY WITH IMPROVEMENTS,
1810 | There has been a ferry at Queensferry for 800 years at least, and the
Scottish King Malcolm III required one to travel from his seat at Dunfermline
to Edinburgh on a regular basis. The ferry was less needed from 1890 when the
cantilever style Forth Railway Bridge was opened, and became obsolete when
the Forth Road Bridge opened in 1964. North and South Queensferry stand
between these two great bridges. It was by reason of its use as a ferry that it had
importance in earlier times and this plan was ordered by the Trustees of the
Town. The plan details the harbour and its defences and notes the land owners,
e.g. Lord Roseberry, Scot Moncrieff, Henry Dundas and the Earl of Morton.
It shows the state of the tide two hours on the flood and other navigational
information. (Admiralty Library Manuscript Collection: Vf 11/8)

THE CARDE OF the
North coaste of England from
Whithye vnto Coket Ile

Stocktō

Gisbroghe

Hartlepoole

Esington

Tees flu.

Redd cliff

Huntley foote

Skelton

Whitbuy

Robinhoodes Bay

NORTH

MERIDIES

ORIENS

4
10
25
20
15
10
25
7
6
40
20
10
10
15
10
28
25
10
20
25
30
35
40
40
40

CHAPTER VII

THE EAST COAST OF
ENGLAND

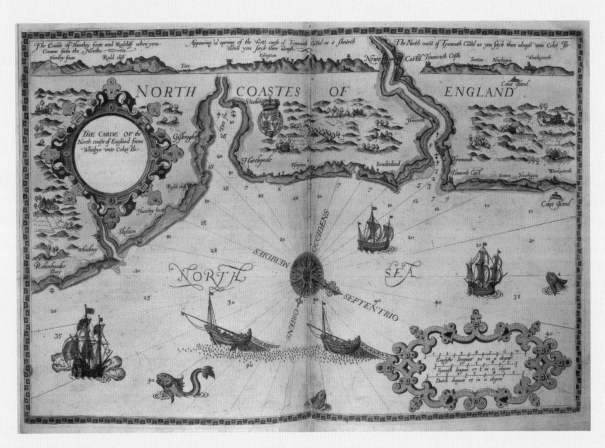

| LEFT DETAIL & ABOVE | CHART OF THE EAST COAST OF ENGLAND FROM COQUET ISLAND TO ROBIN HOOD'S BAY INCLUDING WHITBY AND NEWCASTLE BY LUCAS JANZSOON WAGHENAER, C. 1584 | This is taken from Waghenaer's *Spiegel der Zeevaerdt*. His charts were influenced by the portolan style but had revolutionary new features, with coastal views, a decrease in distance between harbours, bays and rivers, so that these could be enlarged to take information such as depth of water (at half tide), symbols adopted from portolans, such as an anchor for anchorages, a cross for dangerous submerged rocks and dotted areas for sandbanks, and new symbols for navigational buoys and landmarks such as beacons, churches, windmills and rocks awash at half tide. They were the first professional charts compiled by a seaman for use by seamen. (© National Maritime Museum, London, C9515)

'YOUR Roman-Saxon-Danish-Norman English' (from The True-Born Englishman, 1701). Daniel Defoe wrote this pithy description of an Englishman 300 years ago, but it sums up succinctly the influences on the east coast of England. The mix of successive waves of 'immigrants' over the centuries has shaped the coast significantly through the style and scope of edifice, be it port, harbour or village, and by place names and dialect. Coastal erosion is high and in many places the coast is a watery battleground that the sea is winning. The port of Dunwich, for example, that was once on the Suffolk coast is now off it, the houses, wharves and churches now underwater, although it is said the bells can be heard tolling beneath the waves. Conversely, however, around the Norfolk coast and the Wash, new land has been won through the centuries, as enormous embankments allowed drainage of the Fens. But if sea levels continue to rise as a result of global warming, then these areas will be under threat.

The North Sea is frequently a violent sea; its relatively shallow depth and swift water movement generated by tides, prevailing winds and density differences between water masses typically cause steep and high waves with short intervals between wave crests. Defoe described in 1726 how half the houses along the Norfolk coast were built from the wood of shipwrecks and today, in consequence, some 23 lifeboat stations are sited along it, such as those at Cromer and Whitby.

The seaward resources along the east coast are mainly oil and gas, sand and gravel, and fish. Fishing in the North Sea goes back to the Dark Ages and the traditional catch was herring, caught by drift nets at night. Great Yarmouth was once the herring capital of Europe. But with the use of purse seines and mid-water trawls the herring is now exhausted, and, albeit late in the day, a total ban introduced. It remains to be seen how much herring stocks will renew. Flat-fish, which spawn off the coasts of Holland and Belgium, are still caught, but over-fishing is a real problem. The economic salvation of many of the east coast ports and harbours, with attractive old-world towns and beaches, has been as host to, and reliant on, the tourist.

Historically the proximity of the northern coasts did not escape the Vikings' attention in the sixth to ninth centuries, and they first raided and then settled along these coasts, contributing to local names and dialect. The Angles from southern Denmark established the Kingdom of Northumberland, where the coastline has been designated an Area of Outstanding Natural Beauty, with miles of sandy beaches and quiet dunes up to the Scottish border.

A browse along the east coast gives a better understanding of its nature. To explore between Berwick and Amble, where Coquet Island lies offshore, is a restful experience as it alternates between sand dunes and cliffs, but the contrast increases the shock when coming upon the industrialisation south of Amble. Holy Island or Lindisfarne is now an attractive tourist magnet, while the Farne Islands, belonging to the National Trust since 1925, are a magnificent bird sanctuary of 28 islands. The impressive castles of Dunstanburgh on the cliff top overlooking Embleton Bay, and Bamburgh, built round its twelfth-century keep, have been the backdrops for many films. Bamburgh stands 150 feet on a vertical crag of rock, an outcrop of the Whin Sill, itself a seam of dolerite rock that forms part of Hadrian's Wall and appears on Holy Island and in the Farne Islands.

The development of ports around the Tyne during and after the Industrial Revolution changed small fishing hamlets such as South Shields and Blyth into great ports with piers and jetties to export the coal mined in Northumberland, but has left a blight of black coal spoil along the coast.

From the Tyne to Teesdale, which includes heavily populated manufacturing areas around Stockton, Middlesbrough and Hartlepool, the coast is also scarred and blackened by the heavy industries of coalmining, steelworks, oil refineries, chemical plants and power stations. About 12 miles south-east of Redcar at Boulby Head, north of Staithes, itself an attractive fishing village with the oldest part at the cliff-foot and more recent development on the top, is eastern England's highest cliff at 660 feet.

Continuing south is the town of Whitby, best known for its association with the naval explorer and navigator, Captain James Cook, who, as a young merchant seaman learned the skills of sailing and navigating the Whitby cat in one of the most difficult of training nurseries – the North Sea. The town is built on the mouth of the River Esk in two parts, with the east and west headlands embracing the harbour. It has always been a fishing harbour, and Cook's four exploratory ships, the *Endurance*, Resolution, *Adventure* and *Discovery*, were all built here to the same design as the colliers that carried coal up and down the coast. Scarborough, with an impressive headland and castle some 18 miles south of Whitby, has a long history of fishing and shipbuilding, too, and both sea towns offer intriguing medieval streets for the visitor, although Scarborough has additional fame as a spa.

The character of the coast continues to vary. Between Whitby and Scarborough are rocky beaches. Robin Hood's Bay, a cliff-based fishing and smuggling village in days gone by, continuously lost its coast until the sea wall was built in 1975. South of Scarborough at Filey Brigg is an unusual and spectacular formation of lime-rich grit which has remained after softer rocks have been washed away; then south of that are unstable cliffs of boulder clay, eroding fast. Between Filey and Flamborough Head is what many describe as one of Britain's finest stretches of coast with high white chalk cliffs almost smothered in a variety of sea birds, and is today an RSPB reserve. Flamborough Head brings this section of coast to a close with impressive chalk cliffs including stacks, caves and arches.

Continuing on, the coast turns into the crumbling cliffs of Holderness whose name derives from the Viking 'hold', a chieftain, and 'ness', which means a headland, which explains the number of 'nesses' along the east coast of Scotland and England such as Fife Ness or Tarbatness. This coastal stretch of East Yorkshire runs for 35 miles that, with the River Hull as the western boundary, forms a sort of marshland peninsula that extends from Flamborough Head to Spurn Head and along the banks of the River Humber to the south. The constantly changing sand banks around Spurn Head cover the entrance to the River Humber Estuary, crossed by the elegantly poised Humber Road Bridge, built in 1981 with a span of 4626 feet – one of the world's longest single-span suspension bridges. The Humber is the boundary between Yorkshire and Lincolnshire.

Hull developed as a port straddling the River Hull's entrance about 20 miles east of the North Sea into the Humber and has important ferry links to Zeebrugge and Rotterdam. Still Britain's third biggest port, after London and Liverpool, it suffered some of the heaviest bombing in the Second World War and has therefore been greatly rebuilt. The medieval town grew to the west of the river and Hull still has many of the old streets, although the moat was rebuilt as the Queen's Docks in 1778. Hull was the birth-place of William Wilberforce who campaigned tirelessly for the abolition of slavery, which was enforced after the Act of 1833, and by the Royal Navy worldwide during the nineteenth century.

The Humber offers excellent natural access to the North Sea and it was inevitable that a port would develop on the south Humber coast, at the mouth of the River Haven: Grimsby. From its founding in the ninth century by the Danes, through the Middle Ages when it developed into Britain's greatest fishing port, an importer of wine from France and Spain and timber from Norway, with coal from Newcastle, its dramatic growth took place in Victorian times. It had a population in 1801 of 1524 that had grown to 92,000 by 1931, from which time it has stayed static. The river was deepened and the railway brought coal for export from 1848. Starting in the mid nineteenth century six docks were built including the Royal, Alexandra, Union and numbers 1, 2 and 3 fish docks (in 1931), with a complementary expansion in the fishing fleet. Today, as with many east coast ports, fishing has declined, although it hosts the National Fishing Heritage Centre, and other light industries such as plastics, chemicals and engineering have developed. The two lifeboats for the Humber estuary are stationed at Cleethorpes and at Spurn Head.

The coastline again changes along the Lincolnshire coast to one of low soft boulder clay cliffs, sand dunes and mud flats that are no match for the encroaching sea. The seaside town of Skegness was transformed by the railway's arrival and Lord Scarborough, who laid it out with wide streets, attractive parades and public amenities that catered well for the visitor.

The Wash has two main ports, Boston and King's Lynn. Boston is up the River Witham, and was once the busiest port in this part of Lincolnshire. The river silted up in the sixteenth century and was cleared in the eighteenth, but is now more of a tourist attraction. King's Lynn became a major port for wool exports up to the sixteenth century, then with the draining of the Fens, of farm produce and shipbuilding in the eighteenth and nineteenth centuries with the Alexandra and Bentinck Docks being built in 1869 and 1883 respectively. It became an overflow for London, even an evacuee centre in the Second World War, but is also now principally a tourist attraction.

The coast from the Wash continuing eastwards towards Brancaster Bay changes to salt marshes. Nelson's birthplace at Burnham Thorpe, and Clay, were ports until the shoreline moved to leave them isolated. The sand dune systems combined with low-lying marshes are typical of the Norfolk and Suffolk coasts but with nature reserves, such as at Blakeney Point in Norfolk, where the National Trust administers a 1300-acre sanctuary flush with the common and little terns, the latter the largest colony in Britain.

Great Yarmouth grew on a narrow spit of land that deflected the course of the River Yare through sand flats and mud flats, where the herring drifters landed and smoked their catch. It had an active shipbuilding industry although it now services the North Sea oil and gas industries, and operates a ferry to Rotterdam. Bomb damage in the Second World War ruined many of the old cramped alleys known as rows, numbered up to 145. It is now Norfolk's most popular seaside resort and largest town, with two piers dating from the 1850s and a maritime museum for rainy days.

The Stour and Orwell rivers flow into a large estuary where Harwich developed from its origins under the Earls of Norfolk in the thirteenth century, partly as a naval base from which to launch attacks on France and a naval dockyard opened in 1660, from which a tread-wheel crane survives, driven by two men walking inside two wheels. Today it is a major port with ferries to the Hook of Holland, Germany and Scandinavia.

Clacton-on-Sea and Southend-on-Sea have at least one thing in common: they both provide seaside recreation for the Londoner as Essex's answers to Margate. With the railway and a pier, originally opened in 1871, Clacton provides all the entertainment of a brash seaside town, while Southend has the world's longest pier at 1½ miles long.

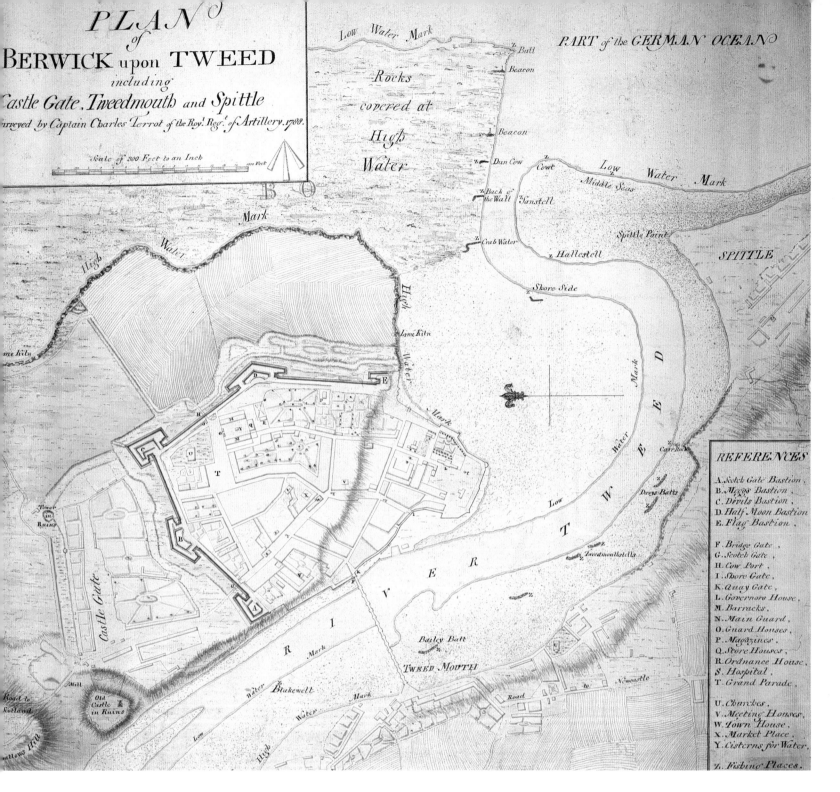

PLAN of BERWICK upon TWEED including Castle Gate, Tweedmouth and Spittle
Surveyed by Captain Charles Terrot of the Roy.! Reg.t of Artillery. 1788.

Scale of 300 Feet to an Inch

PART of the GERMAN OCEAN

Low Water Mark

Rocks covered at High Water

SPITTLE

REFERENCES

A. Scotch Gate Bastion.
B. Meggs Bastion.
C. Devils Bastion.
D. Half Moon Bastion.
E. Flag Bastion.

F. Bridge Gate.
G. Scotch Gate.
H. Cow Port.
I. Shore Gate.
K. Quay Gate.
L. Governors House.
M. Barracks.
N. Main Guard.
O. Guard Houses.
P. Magazines.
Q. Store Houses.
R. Ordnance House.
S. Hospital.
T. Grand Parade.

U. Churches.
V. Meeting Houses.
W. Town House.
X. Market Place.
Y. Cisterns for Water.

Z. Fishing Places.

| PLAN OF BERWICK-UPON-TWEED INCLUDING CASTLE GATE, TWEEDMOUTH AND SPITTLE, SURVEYED BY CAPTAIN CHARLES TERROT OF THE ROYAL REGIMENT OF ARTILLERY, 1788 | Berwick, from the old English meaning 'corn farm', is the northernmost town in England, although logically it should be on the border between England and Scotland, as the border elsewhere follows the River Tweed, which it straddles. Tweedmouth is the seaport. It changed hands between Scotland and England 13 times over the centuries, although it prospered as a wealthy trading port. A traditional poem goes: 'Berwick is an ancient town, a church without a steeple, a pretty girl at every door, and very generous people'. Be that as it may, its citizens have always thought of themselves as neither Scottish nor English but as 'Tweedsiders' or 'Berwickers', although the Scottish influence prevails apart from a Northumberland dialect in their speech. During the Crimean War (1853-6), the declaration of war on Russia was in the name of Great Britain, Ireland and Berwick-upon-Tweed, inferring that without the latter's help, we would not have won! However, Berwick was omitted from the Peace Treaty, and remained technically at war with Russia until 1966 when a ceremonial peace treaty was signed. Berwick was strongly fortified with its town walls (which are still intact), built by Edward I to keep out the Scots. Captain Terrot has included high and low water marks, the forts, fishing places and the prominent beacon and sand banks. (The National Archives {PRO}: MPH 1/228{2})

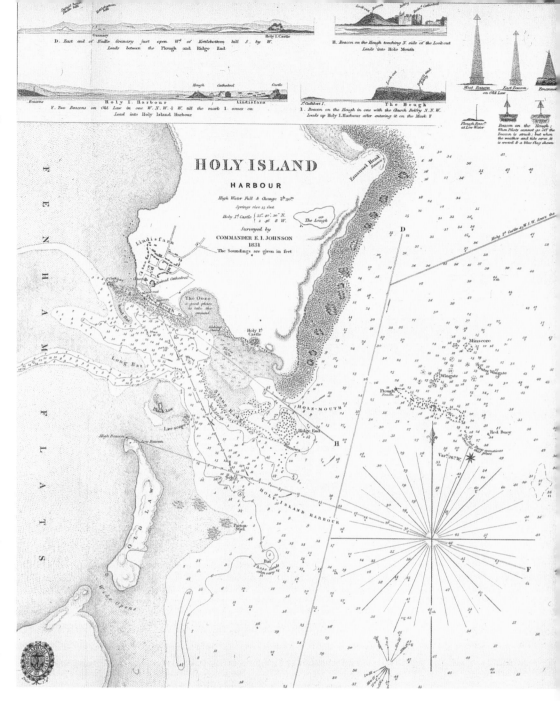

| RIGHT | HOLY ISLAND HARBOUR, SURVEYED BY COMMANDER E J JOHNSON, 1831 | Johnson's chart shows four views of the appearance of the land on the approach, detailed soundings and the high and low beacons in line positioned as guides. He had seen action as a young officer during the Napoleonic War, and in 1818 he joined Captain Martin White's survey ship, Shamrock, off the Irish coast for two years. In 1831 he was ordered by the Admiralty to complete his survey of the Faroe Islands, some 180 miles north of Scotland, which he had started at his own expense when on half-pay (i.e. not employed by the navy). He finished his naval career as the first Superintendent of the Royal Navy Compass Department.

The Hydrographic Office seal, as on this chart, is stamped on all Admiralty charts for what was originally called the Hydrographical Office, and the Admiralty fouled anchor became progressively more embellished over time. It was first applied by hand in 1803, and then incorporated as part of the chart engraving, while the 'al' at the end of Hydrographic was dropped in 1868. The use of Roman numerals as a position indicator for tidal information was by this time standard practice. (Admiralty Library Manuscript Collection: Vy 12/31)

| BELOW | VIEW OF HOLY ISLAND, AND LINDISFARNE ABBEY BY HORATIO N HESS, 1821 | This distinctive view of Holy Island shows Lindisfarne Abbey and St Cuthbert's Island to the left and a beacon along the Heugh. The island was called Holy Island rather than Lindisfarne when, in 1082, the priory, probably built by the same masons as Durham Cathedral in beautiful red sandstone, was run as a Benedictine monastery, although the famous and beautifully illuminated Lindisfarne Gospels, which are kept in the British Library, were written much earlier, around 675. (UKHO © British Crown Copyright)

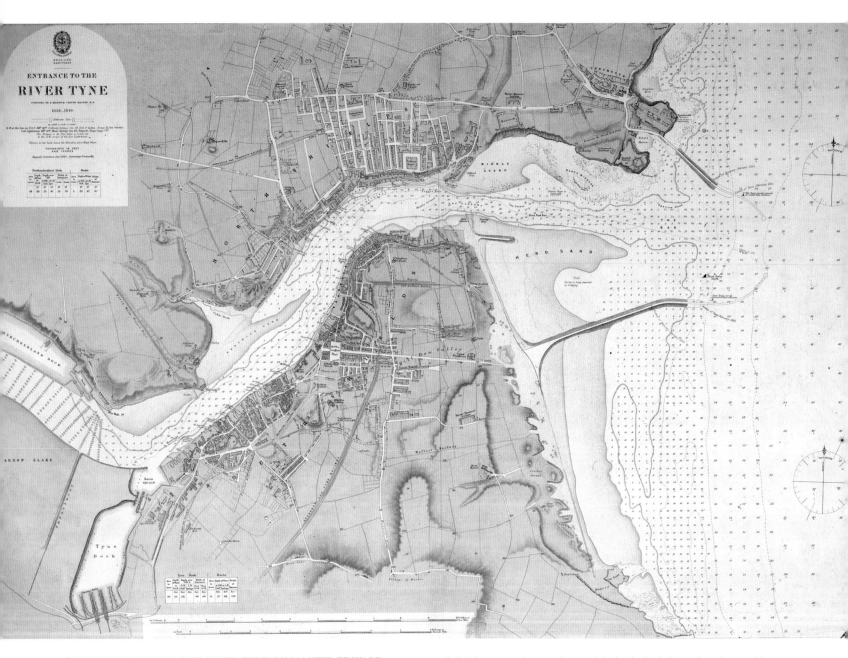

| **THE ENTRANCE TO THE RIVER TYNE BY MASTER EDWARD KILLWICK CALVER, 1838–49** | Calver was to make Staff Commander, but as a Master he commanded HMS *Porcupine*, a paddle-ship, and conducted this important survey of the entrance to the River Tyne. His thorough survey is evident from the neat and prolific lines of soundings, which, in addition to the accuracy of the coast laid down, show a marked difference from the charts of even 50 years before.

The oldest part of Newcastle, now famous for its bridges spanning the River Tyne, is the Quayside, which was, until the nineteenth century, the commercial hub. The principal commodity, coal, had to be loaded into ships that would carry about 300 to 400 tons to London in Northumberland collier brigs like the Whitby cat, similar to the vessel in which Captain James Cook sailed to the Pacific. This was done by highly skilled boatmen, the Keel Men, unique to the north-east, who took their name from their small vessels called keels which could carry around 20 tons of coal. Interestingly the word keel was the first English word ever to be written down, as 'Ceols', the boats in which the Anglo-Saxons invaded Britain in the fifth and sixth centuries (recorded by a Welsh chronicler in the sixth century). (UKHO © British Crown Copyright)

| LEFT | ENGRAVING OF SUNDERLAND, THE WEARMOUTH BRIDGE FROM WESTWARD, BY W H BARTLETT, 1842 | Sunderland is about 7 miles south of Tynemouth, at the mouth of the River Tyne. It has a history of coal exporting and shipbuilding from the first recorded in 1346, with a peak of 99 ships launched in 1903. By 1988 all the Wearside shipyards had closed down.

But like Newcastle's bridges over the Tyne, Sunderland's over the Wear are landmarks and the first iron bridge, shown in this engraving, was the Wearmouth Bridge opened in 1796. The Alexandra Bridge was opened in 1909 and was at that time the heaviest bridge in Britain with a centre span of 2600 tons. Two piers embrace the entrance to the marina and docks, the Roker Pier to the north built in 1903 and the recently completed New South Pier. (By permission of the British Library: 1502/320 Vol. I)

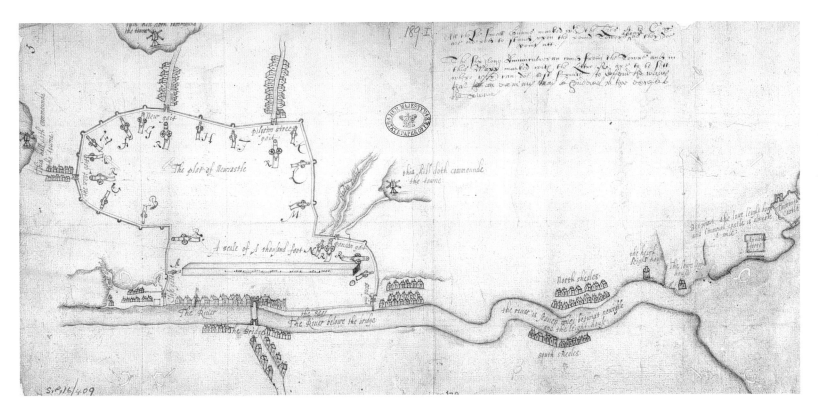

| ABOVE | PLAN OF THE COURSE OF THE RIVER TYNE FROM NEWCASTLE TO THE MOUTH, 1639 | This maritime plan of the River Tyne from Newcastle to the river's mouth is a seventeenth-century snapshot of how it used to be, the purpose of which was to plan improvements on defence. Showing the walls, gates, bastions, armaments, with windmills (visible landmarks from the sea) on the hill commanding the town, it illustrates the course of the River Tyne to the 'German Sea' with notes on the siting of cannon, and on the distance between the low 'leighthouse' and the castle at almost a mile, and 7 miles between Newcastle and the two crude lighthouses. (The National Archives {PRO}: MPF1/287)

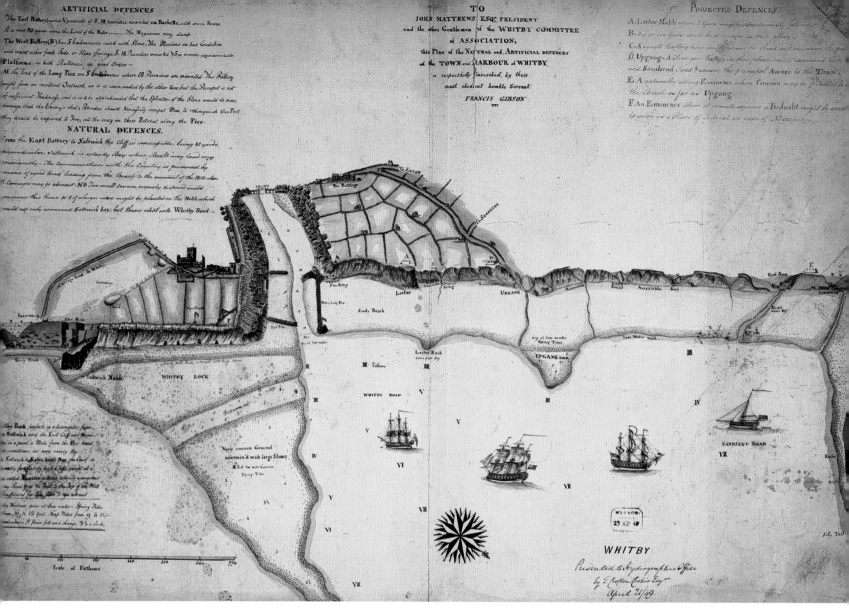

| ABOVE | PORT OF WHITBY BY FRANCIS GIBSON, 1782 | We know
Francis Gibson's profession, as there is an entry from The Times for 15 June 1787
stating: 'Newcastle, June 9th – Last week the Lords of the Treasury appointed Francis
Gibson, Esq. Of Whitby Collector of the Customs in the Port of Whitby…'. There is
an interesting annotation: 'Presented by J. Crofton Croker Esq 1849'. He was the son
of J W Croker, the Secretary to the Admiralty for 22 years from 1809.

Whitby is divided by the River Esk with two piers built out into the North Sea and
a lighthouse on each (disused on the southern one). St Hilda's Abbey high on the East
Cliff dominates the skyline and presents a conspicuous landmark. The river provides
an upper harbour with a marina and lower harbour with fish pier and quay. Whitby
fishermen were involved in whaling for about 80 years from 1750, and once Whitby
had got a lifeboat in 1802 it was engaged in many heroic rescues in the North Sea.
(Admiralty Library Manuscript Collection: Vz 11/29)

| BELOW | VIEW OF THE YORKSHIRE COAST FROM
FLAMBOROUGH HEAD TO ROBIN HOOD'S BAY BY CAPTAIN
WILLIAM HEWETT, 1840 | Hewett has caught more than just the coastline
in this attractive navigational watercolour view with the mood of the March
North Sea wind and sky over the land extending some 35 miles from
Flamborough Head to the Whitby headland just north of Robin Hood's Bay.
There are a number of prominent landmarks identified, including the lighthouse
at Flamborough Head, Dane's Dyke, Filey Point, Red Head, Mount Oliver,
Scarborough Castle and the south and north cheek of Robin Hood's Bay. The
latitude and longitude of each headland or landmark is clearly worked out and
annotated to aid the navigator when consulting the engraved view on the chart.
(UKHO © British Crown Copyright)

MANUSCRIPT PLAN OF SCARBOROUGH AND DEFENCES, C. 1540 | Almost exactly equidistant between Whitby and Flamborough Head is the seaside town and harbour of Scarborough. Unusually it grew not at a river mouth but in the recess of a semicircular sweep of the Yorkshire coast, forming a bay open towards t he south and south-west, protected northwards by a high and steep promontory on top of which the Norman castle was built. It has North Bay on the other side of the promontory. This manuscript plan of Scarborough shows its defences around the time of its siege in 1536 by Robert Aske during the Pilgrimage of Grace, the worst uprising of Henry VIII's reign, which was triggered as a direct result of his anti-Roman Catholic policies and the dissolution of the monasteries. It shows the castle walls with three churches, the oldest, St Mary's, built in 1125, and the town and harbour with warships and fishing boats and the start of the old pier with protective cannon emplaced. A commentary on that time are the four prominent features drawn outside the town (at the bottom of the plan) – the water well, the defence tower by the entrance to the bay, a beacon atop the hill and the hanging gibbet, with body.

In 1620 the wife of the town bailiff, Elizabeth Farrow, discovered the spa waters and it came to rival Harrogate. The visually striking Cliff Bridge opened in 1827 to join the spa with the town by crossing a 400-foot chasm on 75-foot high piers. In 1858 Sir Joseph Paxton had opened a new Spa Hall, and already from 1735 bathing machines were used to sample the sea. (By permission of the British Library: Cotton Augustus I.ii.1)

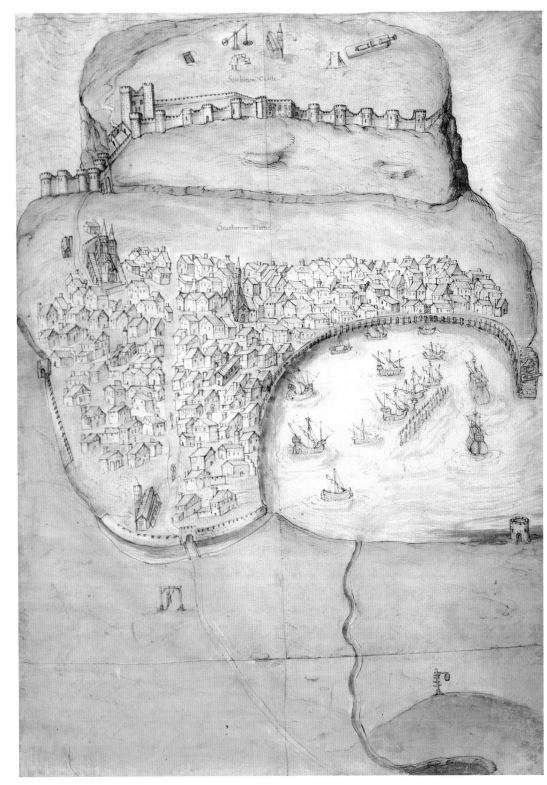

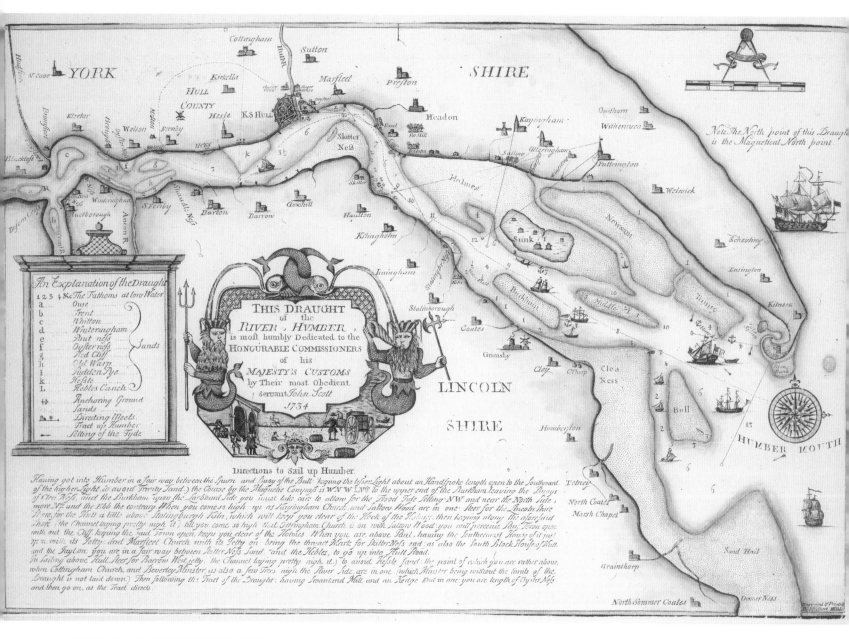

| CHART OF THE RIVER HUMBER WITH SAILING DIRECTIONS BY JOHN SCOTT, 1734 | Drawn in the style of the earlier waggoners, and published privately in response to the Humber's growing importance with a number of ports, the chart was sponsored by and dedicated to the Honourable Commissioners of His Majesty's (then George II) Customs.

The River Humber is the estuary for the a large volume of water draining the Pennines and Yorkshire, Nottingham and Lincolnshire countryside by means of a number of rivers. They include the Derwent, the Ouse, itself fed by the Swale, Ure and Nidd rivers, the Wharfe and Aire, joining to flow through the first Humber port of Goole, and the Trent. Other ports on the estuary are Hull, Immingham and Grimsby. The waters flow out to the North Sea at a 5-mile wide opening bounded by a spit of sand up to 30 feet high, known as Spurn Head, to the north. Such a wide estuary experiences strong tides of up to 4 knots and shifting sandbanks, to the extent that Sunk Island (then in the middle of the river) is now part of the mainland. A narrow but ever-changing buoyed entrance and exit channel for deep-draught vessels, the Hawke and Sunk Channels, are kept open to the north of the estuary. (UKHO © British Crown Copyright)

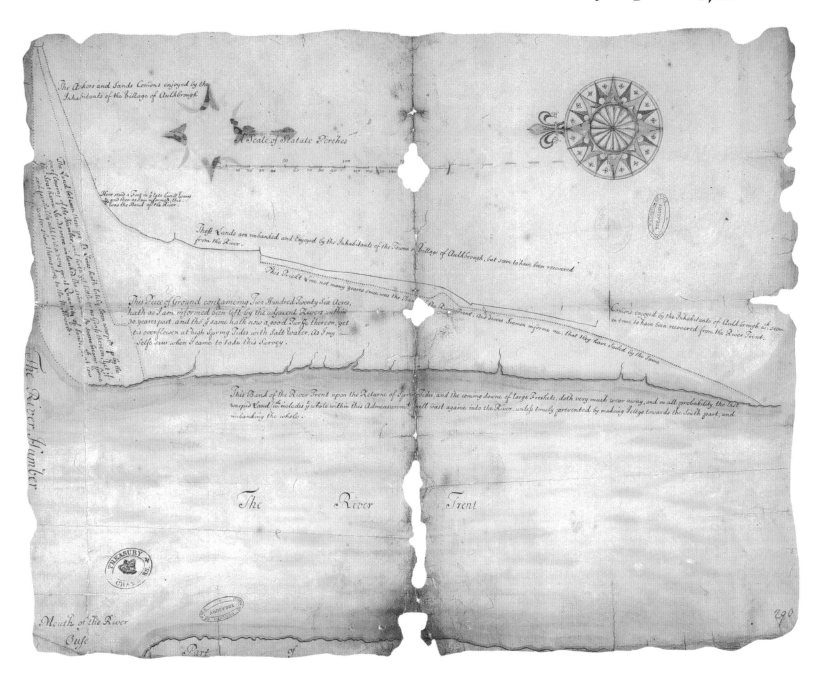

| A SURVEY OF AN AREA OF AND NEAR ALKBOROUGH BETWEEN
THE RIVERS TRENT AND HUMBER THAT IS NOW DRY LAND,
SHOWING ORIGINAL SHORELINES, AND NOTES ON NATURE
AND QUALITY OF LAND, 1704 | Alkborough is still a small but isolated
village of around 500 residents near the northern end of the cliff range of hills
overlooking the point named Trent Falls, where the Trent and Ouse Rivers join to
form the Humber. This survey of an area around Alkborough is now dry land, but
shows the original shorelines, with notes on the nature and quality of land, which
gives an idea of how the eastern coast is changing over time.

The plan itself shows, with a beautiful compass rose, the 'Akers and Sands
Comons enjoyed by the Inhabitants of the Village'. The labyrinth cut into the turf
in one of these 'akers' in at least medieval times (the first written mention is in
1697) is known as Julian's Bower and, fortunately, still survives. (The National
Archives {PRO}: MFQ1/268)

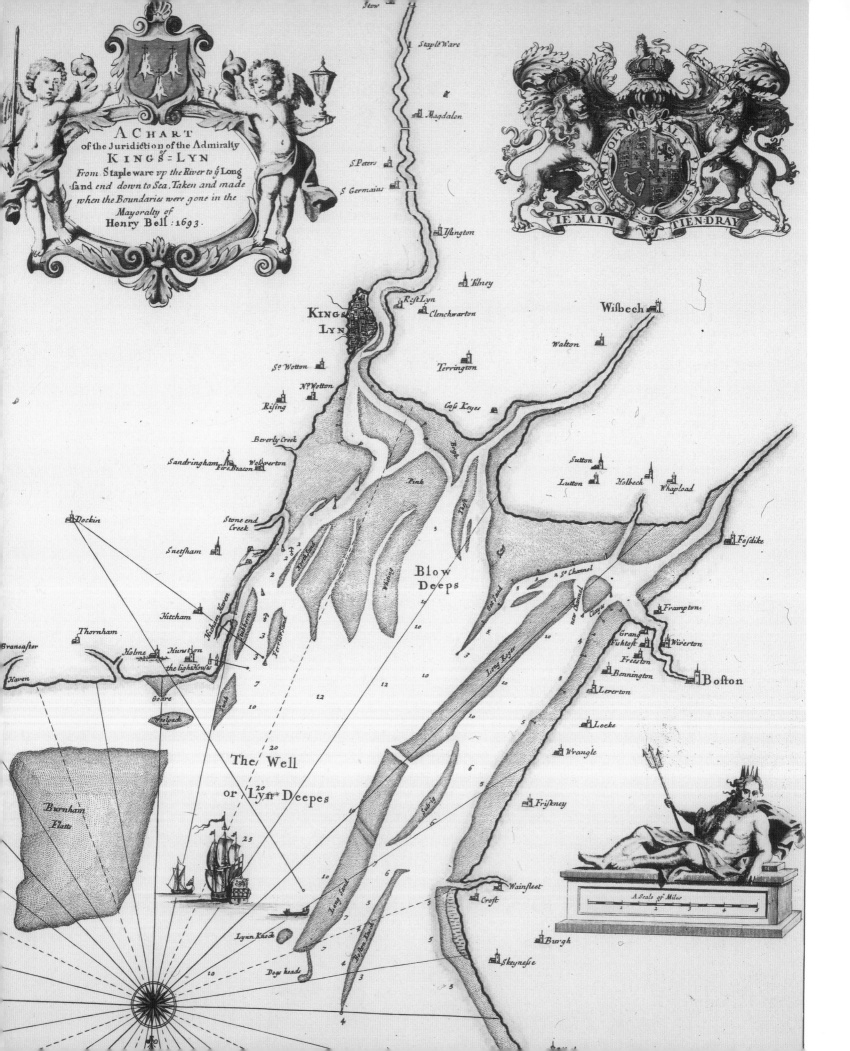

A CHART
of the Jurifdiction of the Admiralty
of KINGS=LYN
From Staple ware vp the River to y Long
Iſand end down to Sea, Taken and made
when the Boundaries were gone in the
Mayoralty of
Henry Bell : 1693.

IE MAIN   DIEN·DRAY

Stow
Staple Ware
Magdalen
S. Peters
S. Germains
Iſlington
Tilney
KINGS LYN
Wiſbech
R. S.t Lyn
Clenchwarton
Walton
S.t Wotton
Terrington
N.d Wotton
Croſs Keyes
Riſing
Sutton
Beverly Creek
Lutton   Holbech   Whapload
Sandringham   Wolverton
Fire Beacon
Pink
Dockin
Stone end Creek
Fosdike
Snetfham
Blow Deeps
Hitcham
Frampton
Thornham
Wiverton
Brancaſter
Holme   Hunſton
the lightHowſe
Grand Sutost
Freeſton
Bennington   Boſton
Haven
Goare
Leverton
Loeke
The Well
or Lyn Deepes
Wrangle
Burnham Flatts
Friſkney
Wainfleet
Croft
Burgh
Lynn Knock
Skeyneſse
Dogs heade

A Scale of Miles

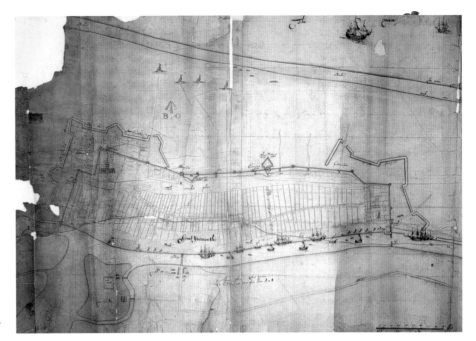

| OPPOSITE | A CHART OF KING'S LYNN, BY C MERIT, 1693 | The name Lynn means 'pool' in Celtic, and King's Lynn in Norfolk is sited on the River Ouse at the south-eastern part of the large North Sea estuary, the Wash. It was originally called Bishop's Lynn, but when Henry VIII took the Lordship (and a lot more off the church besides) it became King's Lynn. The pleasing chart has North oriented to the bottom of the page and contains the royal coat of arms of William III, distinguished by the lion of the House of Orange in the centre with the arms of King's Lynn depicted in the top left corner.

The sands in the Wash are constantly shifting and any pilot, such as Reed's Nautical Almanac or the Admiralty Pilot, will tell you to contact the local harbourmaster before entering to check the current situation. Towards the end of the seventeenth century as commercial maritime activity grew, so too did demand for charts, and numerous surveys like this were made of many English harbours. King's Lynn was of considerable importance at the time since a large proportion of the trade of the Eastern Counties, both with continental Europe and with other parts of England, was engaged in this port. The chart still reflects the influence of the waggoners, but it is the first chart of the Wash to show the banks and channels in any useful detail. (UKHO © British Crown Copyright)

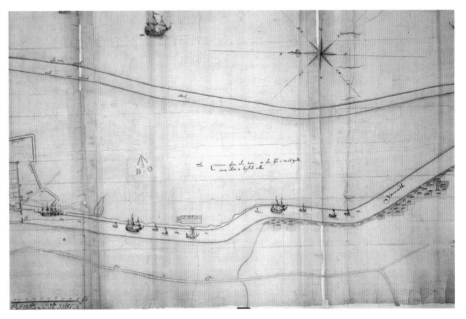

| RIGHT | MAP OF GREAT YARMOUTH AND THE RIVER YARE BY SIR BERNARD DE GOMME, 1666 | De Gomme came to England with Prince Rupert (actually Count Palatine of the Rhine and Duke of Bavaria), Charles I's nephew, who fought as his hot-headed, but often brilliant, cavalry commander during the Civil War in 1642. De Gomme rose to Engineer-in-Chief in 1661 and Surveyor-General of Ordnance in 1682.

His survey (depicted here in three parts), which shows a busy River Yare with many ships running up and down with the fort at Spurn, the walled and fortified town and St Nicholas Church, includes some intriguing historical detail; 'The Bouling Greene', town lanes only '6 foot broad', a new planned town 'from A to B' by Sir Robert Preston, a lime kiln on the south bank, a windmill to the north, salt pans to the east, all to a scale of 300 yards, 900 feet to an inch with 1760 yards in an English mile. (The National Archives {PRO}: 1/487)

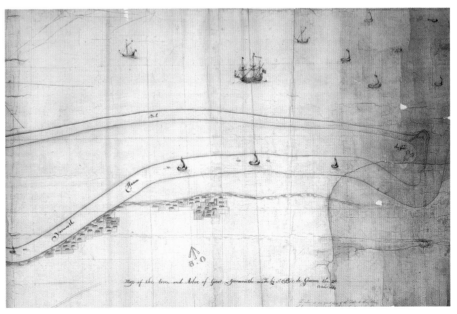

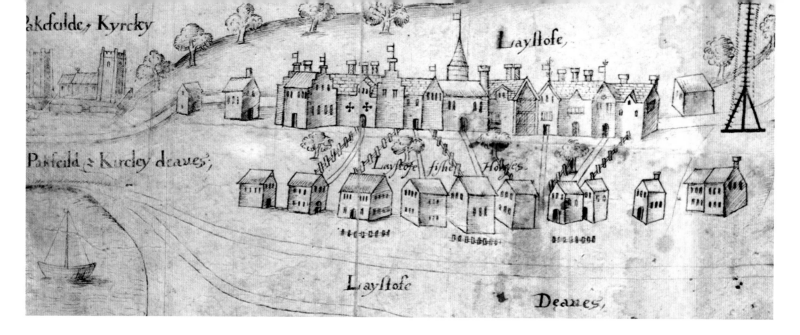

| ABOVE | VIEW OF LOWESTOFT FROM THE SEA, 1580 | The detail from this map of the Manor of Gunton, gives one of the very earliest views of Lowestoft from the sea, and came about because it was, apparently, executed in the case between a John Hoo, tenant of Lowestoft Manor, and a Robert Wroote, owner of Gunton 1579–80.

Lowestoft, situated on top of coastal cliffs in Suffolk at the mouth of the River Waveney, was a small medieval fishing town. It was developed by Sir Morton Peto, the 'maker of Lowestoft', in early Victorian times, with the opening of the railway connection to Norwich and the herring catch (known as 'silver darlings') was sent to markets such as London. Lowestoft was bombed during the Second World War, destroying the old Grove Estate which has been substantially rebuilt, but the 'Scores', or old harbour lanes, survive. Today the harbour is entered between the north and south piers giving access to Waveney and Hamilton Docks to the north and, by the yacht basin, home to the Royal Norfolk and Suffolk Yacht Club and a trawl basin, access to the Norfolk Broads. (By permission of the British Library: ADD.56070)

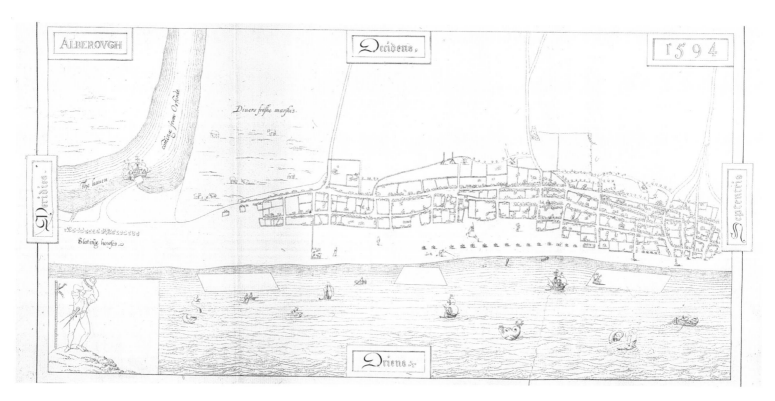

| ABOVE | PLAN OF ALDEBURGH, 1594 | Benjamin Britten set up a lasting legacy here with the annual music festival. This plain map of the coast and town give an insight as to how it was in the sixteenth century, when fishing and small boat building were the chief activities, with boats hauled up the shingle beaches. Local fishermen still offer their catch and the area is renowned for its wild bird life. You can sail a 10-mile voyage in a small boat up the River Ore, entering from Hollesley Bay, which flows behind a spit of land parallel to the sea, becoming the River Alde, which comes down from Snape, past the Wildlife Reserves at Minsmere, run by the RSPB, and Havergate Island. The sand bar at the entrance shifts a lot after storms, and the overfalls around Orfordness reach 6 knots at spring tides. The Pilot's advice: 'do not enter before half flood or at night' should be heeded. Centuries ago the port of Slaughten was washed away by the sea, and six streets from the town have been lost to the sea through coastal erosion since this chart was made. (Admiralty Library Manuscript Collection: Vz 11/1)

| MANUSCRIPT PLAN OF HARWICH HARBOUR BY SIR PIERCY BRETT, 1754 | Harwich, with the actually older Dovercourt, was first known of as a sea port in 1150, and protrudes out into the North Sea at the estuary of the Orwell and Stour rivers. On the opposite promontory is Felixstowe with a deep-water channel dredged for the ferries. The estuary offers the only safe anchorage between the Thames and Humber. The town grew in the seventeenth century to harbour cod fishermen and import coal from Newcastle, while Harwich seamen were prominent in the New World colonies. Towards the end of the seventeenth century the packet boat service began and during the eighteenth century Harwich prospered. However, in the nineteenth century the packet boat service transferred to Tilbury with its railway and Harwich's fishing activity diminished. The Ha'penny Pier was built in 1853 and the railway service began in the following year.

Harwich, ideally placed to cover the North Sea and Continental naval bases, was much used by the Royal Navy in the two World Wars as a destroyer and submarine base, and was where the German U-boats surrendered in 1918.

Brett was one of Admiral Lord Anson's lieutenants during the famous raiding circumnavigation of 1740–44. His drawings of the epic voyage show his talent and he had also drawn charts en route. This chart is effectively a survey to assess the defence of Harwich in 1754 and Brett shows Fort Landguard on 'The Andrews' and, of domestic importance for troops and ships, the leaden pipes bringing spring water to the town. He has put red figures for the shoals in feet and black figures in the channels in fathoms at low water. (Admiralty Library Manuscript Collection: Vz 11/5)

| CHART OF ORFORDNESS, 1588 | This early chart dates to the year of the Spanish Armada and comes from Lord Burghley's State Papers. It shows the coast from Bawdsey, including Orfordness and Aldeburgh and the complex river arrangement, to Thorpeness. (By permission of the British Library: ADD.11802.N)

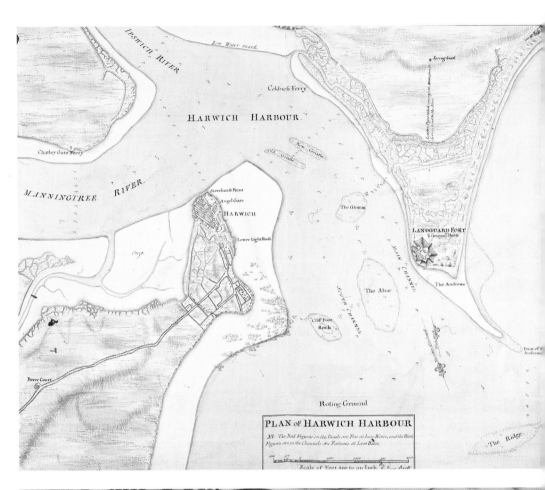

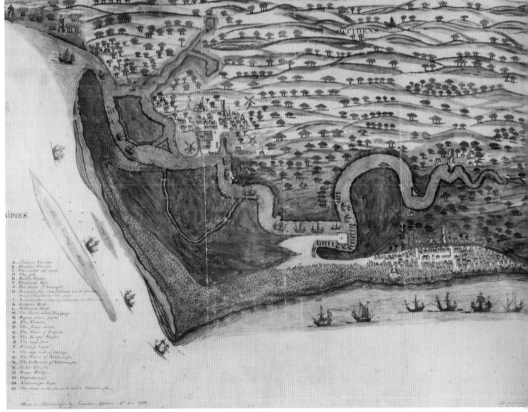

Bibliography

Admiralty Charts and Publications, *Admiralty Distance Tables*, NP350, 1978

Admiralty Charts and Publications, *Admiralty Ocean Passages for the World*, NP136, 4th Edition 1987

Admiralty Charts and Publications, *The Mariner's Handbook*, NP100, 1979

Admiralty Charts and Publications, *The Sea Pilot*, various volumes

Admiralty Hydrographic Department, *Admiralty Manual of Hydrographic Surveying*, 1938

Admiralty Hydrographic Department, 'Professional Paper 13', London, 1950

Bathurst, Bella, *The Lighthouse Stevensons*, HarperCollins, 1999

Bragg, Melvyn, *The Adventure of English*, Hodder & Stoughton, 2003

Campbell, Tony, 'Portolan Charts From the Late Thirteenth Century to 1500', *The History of Cartography*, Vol. 1, edited by J B Hartley and David Woodward, Chicago, 1987

Cavendish, Richard, *Explore Britain's Coastline*, The AA, 1994

Charnock John, *Biographia Navalis*, late eighteenth century

Courtney, Nicholas, 'Gale Force 10', *Review*, 2002

Crane, Nicholas, *Mercator, The Man Who Mapped the Planet*, Weidenfeld & Nicolson, 2002

Crone G R, *Maps and Their Makers*, Hutchinson & Co; Publishers Ltd, 1953

Cunliffe, Tom, *Celestial Navigation*, Fernhurst Books, 1989

Dawson, Cdr L S, *Memoirs of Hydrography*, Henry Keay, 1885

Day, Vice-Admiral Sir Archibald, *The Admiralty Hydrographic Service*, HM Stationery Office, 1967

Defoe, Daniel, *A Tour Through the Whole Island of Great Britain*, Everyman's Library, 1928 (originally published 1724–6)

Dillon, Paddy, *Exploring the South of Ireland*, Ward Lock, 1998

Douwma, Robert, 'Admiralty Charts and Selected Maps', Catalogue 28, 1984

Featherstone, Neville, and Lambie, Peter, *Reed's Oki Nautical Almanac*, Adlard Coles Nautical, 2004

Fisher, Susanna, 'Address at the 54th AGM of the Royal Institute of Navigation', 25th October 2000

Fisher Susanna, *History of the Blueback Chart*, Imray, Laurie, Norie & Wilson Ltd, 2001

Freeman, John, *The Coasts of Britain*, Bison Books Ltd, 1985

Freethy Ron, *The Naturalist's Guide to the British Coastline*, David & Charles, 1983

Greeves, Lydia and Trinick, Michael, *The National Trust Guide*, National Trust Enterprises Ltd, 1966

The History of Cartography, Vol. I, University of Chicago Press, 1987

HM Stationery Office, *Admiralty Manual of Navigation*, Volumes II and III, 1955

The Haven-finding Art, Cambridge University Press, first published 1956, augmented edition 1971

Hayter, Alethea, *The Wreck of the Abergavenny*, Macmillan, 2002

Houghton, David, *Weather at Sea*, Fernhurst Books, 1986

Howse, Derek & Sanderson, Michael, *The Sea Chart*, David & Charles, 1973

Kemp, Peter, *The Oxford Companion to Ships and the Sea*, Oxford University Press, 1976

King, Dean, *A Sea of Words*, Henry Holt and Company, first edition, 1995

Knight, Christopher and Butler, Alan, *Civilisation One*, Watkins, 2004

Lavery, Brian, *Nelson's Navy*, Conway Maritime Press, 1989

Letters and Papers of Henry VIII, XIV (i) no. 732, *John Dee General and Rare Memorials Pertaining to the Perfect Arte of Navigation* (1577 edition)

Manley, John, *Atlas of Prehistoric Europe*, Phaidon Press Ltd, 1989

Natkiel, Richard & Preston, Antony, *Atlas of Maritime History*, Bison Books Ltd, 1986

Neill, Kenneth, *An Illustrated History of the Irish People*, Dublin, 1979

Norman, R, *The Newe Attractive*, London, 1581

Richardson W A R, 'An Elizabethan Pilot's Charts (1594)' ex-RIN paper, The Flinders University of Australia

Ritchie, Rear-Admiral G S, *The Admiralty Chart*, Hollis & Carter Ltd, 1967

Ritchie, Rear-Admiral Steve, *As It Was*, GITC, 2003

Rodger, N A M, *The Wooden World*, Collins, 1986

Sider, Sandra, *Maps, Charts, Globes: Five Centuries of Exploration*, The Hispanic Society of America, 1992

Stefoff, Rebecca, *The British Library Companion to Maps and Mapmaking*, The British Library, 1995

Taylor, E G R, *Mathematics and the Navigator in the 13th Century*, Institute of Navigation, 1980

The Times Concise Atlas of the World, Times Books, 1993

Wallis, Helen & Tyacke, Sarah (Eds), *My Head is a Map*, Francis Edwards and Carta Press, 1973

Wallis Dr Helen, 'The Rotz Atlas: A Royal Presentation', *The Map Collector*, Issue No. 20 Sept 1982

Waters, David, *Art of Navigation*, Part III, National Maritime Museum, 1978

Williams, Glyn, *The Prize of all the Oceans*, HarperCollins, 1999

Wilson, Philip, *The National Maritime Museum*, Philip Wilson and Summerfield Press Ltd, 1982

Woolley, Benjamin, *The Queen's Conjuror: The Life and Magic of Dr Dee*, HarperCollins, 2002

Index

Page references in **bold** indicate maps and captions; those in *italics* indicate illustrations